TRANSFIGURED

SCROLLS FROM HEAVEN

SANCTIONED LOVE
LYNDA RENNE MINISTRIES

STALDER
BOOKS & PUBLISHING LLC

Cover art by Emma Sturm
Published by Stalder Books & Publishing, LLC

For prayer requests, to book an event, or for questions contact:
Sanctioned Love Ministries
PO BOX 7478
Klamath Falls, OR 97602
Visit the author's website at www.SanctionedLove.com

Trade Paperback ISBN 978-0-578-64526-1

First Edition: July 2020

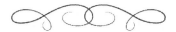

WITH HUMBLE HEARTS, WE DEDICATE THIS BOOK
TO THE BEST TEACHER OF ALL:

THE HOLY SPIRIT.

CONTENTS

PRAISE FOR
Sanctioned Love and
Transfigured Scrolls from Heaven

"Sanctioned Love is a beautiful collective of laid-down lovers of Jesus. Each one has a personal, profound connection with Him in secret. They so beautifully minister God's heart as a cohesive team. What they carry brings light into darkness, awakens the Bride to her true purpose, and unapologetically unearths the gold in people. Personally, I've witnessed them moving in the power of the Spirit. I accepted an invitation to join their team for a planning retreat. They honored me richly, and I was immensely blessed as they ministered by the Spirit to awaken long-standing purposes and promises of God in my life. My ministry team in North Carolina has been so blessed as they have faithfully encouraged and prayed us through transitions, gatherings, and international mission trips. I'm honored to call them friends for life. Sanctioned Love is a team of women who pray much and are deep wells of wisdom and the Word. I would highly recommend them as ministers of Spirit and truth."

—RIVERA DOUTHIT, author and founder of
Rivera International Ministries

"We were so blessed to have Lynda Renne and Sanctioned Love minister to our Love Says Go Ministries leadership team this year. I was so impressed with how much time and preparation in prayer Lynda and her team had invested into our team before they actually ministered to us. When we met them, it was as if they already "knew" us. That was special.

The actual ministry time was so incredible, and unlike anything I have experienced before. Over the years, we have experienced many great prophetic moments of encouragement. Still, I have never seen a team work together as we witnessed Sanctioned Love flowing harmoniously together in the Spirit. Each person on the team brought a special anointing and personality to the prophetic flow, and each word seemed to be built upon the previous one. The presence of God was so rich and thick that one of my team members said it had been years since she felt this much of God in a room.

There were so many specific words of knowledge the Holy Spirit gave them that it was uncanny. Three people gave "worship" words to Bruno, the worship leader, not knowing anything about him. Another word was given about "government" to Sandy, who works for the US government.

I could go on and on about how specific these words were to our team.

I do not remember having cried, laughed, and been on such an amazing roller coaster ride of God's love, presence, and prophetic truth in a ministry setting. It took me and our leadership team days and possibly a couple of weeks to start to unpack this amazing gift that Sanctioned Love imparted to us. It is months later, and we are still reviewing and are being refreshed by the words they gave us. This ministry time brought us closer as a team. It was so refreshing and encouraging to really believe and trust God for "the more."

It is a great joy to recommend Lynda Renne and Sanctioned Love to the highest degree. Their professionalism, quality of heart, care, and anointing was stellar from start to finish.

One last comment: If you are so blessed to have Sanctioned Love minister with you, please do not merely bring regular boxes of tissue; you most likely will need rolls of paper towels to absorb the beautiful tears of joy."

—JASON CHIN, author and founder of
Love Says Go Ministries International

This ministry is one that possesses great transformation for those seeking a deeper walk and greater revelation of the love of our Heavenly Father. All of the team members of this powerful ministry have worked together for many years and have amazing unity and spiritual cohesiveness. Their passion to see lives transformed, healed, delivered and set free is paramount. They all work in the giftings of the Holy Spirit with reverence and honor. Their prophetic gifting is extremely pronounced and wonderfully accurate.

I highly endorse and recommend this ministry and its team. Any leader desiring to see a breakthrough in the spirit within their church or people should have Sanctioned Love as soon as possible.

—REV. JAMES BOYD, Refuge City Church

FOREWORD

By Nanette Oleson

My first introduction to the Sanctioned Love team was when my friend, Melissa, reached out and told me about a group she ministered with called Sanctioned Love. She insisted that I meet this amazing group of women, so I happily agreed to host a "garden party" and invited friends, church leaders, and neighbors for a refreshing time of ministry in the outdoor setting of my yard.

Sanctioned Love set up stations where people encountered the presence of the Holy Spirit through prophesy, teaching, art, and music. The anointing of God's presence was palpable. From that time forward, I knew this tribe was my dearest kin from the Father of Love.

Most of the people who attended the party, like myself, longed for the manifest presence of God. After almost 50 years of pursuing God, only fresh manna can satisfy. Without sounding prideful, after such a lengthy journey, you come to a place where your deepest cry is to experience the very heart of Jesus. Only the manifest beauty of the Holy Spirit truly impels you. Sanctioned Love carried such an anointing, hosting the heart of God and doling it out like freshly baked bread, manna from heaven. Testimonies poured in for days after the party along with invitations from pastors asking the Sanctioned Love ministry team to host women's retreats and speaking engagements.

A global organization, Love Says Go, requested that Sanctioned Love come to Bethel Church in Redding, California, and minister to this group gathering internationally and from all around the United States. While the phrase "Love Says Go," has been coined by another ministry, it aptly applies to Sanctioned Love. Recently, a large church retreat cancelled a 3-day engagement due to the Coronavirus pandemic, but the team still traveled to minister to a tiny congregation of fifteen people in a farming town whose hungry cry said, "Come anyway."

Their unified "yes" to each other and the Lord has brought the team to Cambodia, India, and Rescue Missions. They are living examples of people who give all to touch one. The power behind Sanctioned Love is their unyielding commitment to walk and live together in unity. I have heard it several times from leaders including my lifetime friend, Theresa Dedmon—who has a global ministry to release God's creativity in the marketplace—that Sanctioned Love's unity of purpose and clarity of prophetic insight is unlike any other ministry.

When meetings are scheduled, the team fervently prays for each name, preparing their hearts to impart fresh revelation and love. Sanctioned Love's unity in the Spirit provides the impetus for powerful, prophetic prayer that seems to soak into the fibers and DNA of the recipient.

Since my initial encounter with the team, I've had many welcome experiences seeing Sanctioned Love minister to churches, conferences, pastoral leaders, even trafficked girls and lepers from India. There is nothing cookie-cutter about the way they minister, and their touch is always life-changing.

My friends from Sanctioned Love are fearless lovers of Jesus and people who continually chase after the heart of God. When I was asked to read the manuscript for *Transfigured Scrolls from Heaven*, I honestly did not expect to be moved to such an extent. I immediately shared a few of the writings with friends knowing the content would profoundly reverberate hope into their present situation, like a deep massage that soaks into the tissues and penetrates the spiritual man.

This collection is filled with a rare, honest truth that expresses the beauty and emotion of passionate hearts longing for an authentic relationship with the Father, His Son, and the Holy Spirit. This book is a delightful banquet of poems, stories, and personal reflections originating from Sanctioned Love's vulnerable journey to uncover the truth about God's perspective. They share their life-lessons with honesty and a personal flair. It includes twelve different individual's perspectives as they communicate a wide range of topics including gratitude, grief, acceptance, and identity. It is our hope that you will thoroughly enjoy the homespun flavor, variety, and profound depth of these writings.

INTRODUCTION

By Lynda Renne, president & founder of Sanctioned Love

The birthing of Lynda Renne Ministries and Sanctioned Love began several years ago when I attended a prayer conference in Brooklyn Park, Minnesota, in the late 1990s. I had such a hunger and thirst for God that I pressed into the strong leading of the Holy Spirit that had compelled me to travel farther than I had ever traveled before. Little did I know that this adventure was about to change the course of my life forever.

I recall an evening service during the prayer conference that ended with an invitation to come to the altar. That same hunger and deep craving in my heart that had led me to this conference, caused me to run into the Father's presence with a burning cry to know more of Him. There, on the steps, I lay sobbing as the Father encountered me. His love washed over me with a greater transformation and definition of the purpose He had for my life from that moment on.

As I lay there, I was caught up into a spiritual realm that I had never known or experienced before—nor can I explain it—and ever since that day, the Father speaks directly to my heart.

When His presence lifted, I found myself still lying on the steps while the worship leader was softly playing from a grand piano, even though everyone else had left. That was such a comfort to me.

Hours had passed while I had been in the Spirit with the Lord, hearing Him speak His Word into my heart and rejoicing in His love. My Heavenly Father knew my heart better than anyone, and He set me free to begin the mission of Isaiah 61:1-4. To mend broken hearts and bring those who are lost and broken, into His presence. He blessed me with His grace when He told me, *"I'm going to give you a company of women and you will travel, preach, and teach the love of God to all you encounter."* These women He spoke of would accompany me on this journey during this lifetime. This company has become known as Sanctioned Love.

Each one of these Jesus-loving women carries a beautiful soul and a passion to share their stories so that others can grow in their relationship with God. This team that God entrusted to me has become "my tribe," my co-laborers, and covenant partners. We are connected by a deep-rooted thread of love for our Heavenly Father.

Many years later, while in a moment of prayer seeking the Lord for the team, I heard the Father say, *"I want the scrolls of Sanctioned Love's hearts to be read."*

Upon hearing His voice, I saw a vision. There, upon my heart, sat a rolled-up piece of parchment paper like a scroll, and the bottom of this scroll was unrolled slightly, just a few inches, revealing a transcription that I knew in my heart was written from parts of my life.

Suddenly, an angel appeared and stood next to me on my left side. Great joy and excitement projected from him, yet he remained silent. Without a word, he leaned forward and placed his index finger on the scroll that was upon my heart. At the moment of contact, it unwound into an elegant flowing crimson dress with swirling sentences written across the fabric, one after another until beautiful calligraphy decorated the entire dress and down the length of the train. That beautiful swirling calligraphy represented the hearts of Sanctioned Love, all of which were intertwined with mine.

Once again, I heard His powerful voice as my Heavenly Father repeated, *"I want the scrolls of their hearts to be read."*

This magnificent image was the answer to an impression that I had been holding within my heart, one I had heard from God earlier. Sanctioned Love was embodied within this vision.

All of the scrolls had become one, representing our unity.

The crimson red was the power of the blood, which unified us.

The stories of our hearts that are scribed within the pages of this book are from the heart of the Father, and He wants these stories to be read.

I find such joy to have this kind of fellowship with my God and King. I trust Him, and in obedience to Him, we submit these scrolls from our hearts to you, the reader. We hope this book will draw you into a conversation with God.

All who have authored in this book feel as though it is a work of art, a decorated tale. A tale created by our struggles, our questions, our unanswered prayers, and even our answered prayers. Each of us, unique in our language with God, share our personal testimonies in hopes that they will give you some insight into the scrolls written from our hearts.

We hope that our journey invites greater freedom to receive this truth: that you have, and always will be, pursued by His love.

Let Him write His scroll on your heart. May it, too, become a decorated tale.

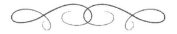

*T*he Spirit of the Lord is upon me, because the Lord has anointed and qualified me to preach the Gospel of good tidings to the meek, the poor and afflicted; He has sent me to bind up and heal the brokenhearted, to proclaim liberty to the [physical and spiritual] captives and the opening of the prison and of the eyes to those who are bound. To proclaim the acceptable year of the Lord [the year of His favor] and the day of vengeance of our God, to comfort all who mourn. To grant [consolation and joy] to those who mourn in Zion---to give them an ornament (a garland or diadem) of beauty instead of ashes, the oil of joy instead of mourning, the garment [expressive] of praise instead of a heavy, burdened, and failing spirit---that they may be called oaks of righteousness [lofty, strong and magnificent, distinguished for uprightness, justice, and right standing with God], the planting of the Lord that He may be glorified. And they shall rebuild the ancient ruins; they shall raise up the former desolations and renew the ruined cities, the devastations of many generations.

Isaiah 61:1-4 AMPC

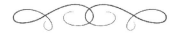

LYNDA RENNE

When I was 11 years old, I remember sitting on the edge of my sister Kathleen's bed. She had been radically saved in the 70s during the Jesus movement, and seeing how much she loved Jesus, I was drawn to her pure passion and new freedom that she had found in this Savior named Jesus.

While we were sitting there together, she asked me if I wanted to ask Jesus to be my Lord and Savior. Right then and there, I felt a deep yearning to surrender my life and learn all I could about Him. Without hesitation, I said, "YES!"

Shortly after accepting Jesus, I began attending a Spirit-filled adult Bible study in the Catholic church with my mother. Even though I was the youngest one there, I was in such awe and wonder wanting to know everything I could about Jesus because He had captured my heart.

The kind gentleman who led the Bible study asked if I wanted to receive the Baptism of the Holy Spirit with the evidence of speaking in tongues. I said "Yes!" and in that second, the language of heaven became my new native tongue. He began to prophesy over me. He said that I would preach the gospel, I would love extremely deeply, and this intense love would cause pain and heartache; it would be a thorn of love all the days of my life. A thorn that would pierce my heart, allowing God's love to penetrate deeper into my heart, allowing me to love others more deeply.

Though I've had many broken times, I have seen the faithfulness of my Heavenly Father through it all. He has always been faithful. I have experienced His divine recompense strongly in my life and the redeeming love of Jesus Christ. He has placed a holy written word on my scroll that has lit a fire in my belly. This propels me with a great passion to know the deep and sacred places in the Father's heart.

To know Him is to crave Him. My heart longs for the adoration and affection of the face-to-face connection with my King and to understand the Holy Spirit in the fullness of His presence upon my life. My testimony has always been: to die is to gain (Philippians 1:21.) To die to myself is to gain Christ and to know Him and His heart in the depths of my being. Ultimately, I have gained a deeper intimacy with my Savior. I can genuinely say He is the lover of my soul.

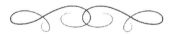

OUR "YES" CAN COST US SOMETHING

Then King David said to Ornan, "No, but I will surely buy it for the full price,
for I will not take what is yours for the Lord,
nor offer burnt offerings with that which cost me nothing.
1 Chronicles 21:24 NKJ

King David had sinned against the Lord, resulting in a plague throughout Israel. David repented before the Lord and desired to build an alter to offer a sacrifice to the Lord, his God. Ornan offered to give King David the field and the threshing floor for free, along with oxen and everything King David needed for his sacrifice. But worship should not be cheap. A sacrifice that costs nothing is not a sacrifice. King David said to Ornan, *"No, I insist on paying full price. I will not take for the Lord what is yours or sacrifice a burnt offering that cost me nothing."* (1 Chronicles 21:24.) It was important to King David to pay the full price of the field. To take another man's goods to offer as a sacrifice to the Lord would have been theft and not acceptable to God.

We can come casually, or fully into worshiping and serving our King. Are you half-hearted or all in? There is a price on our flesh as we are presented with the choices of heaven, opportunities to go all in with Jesus.

We have free access to all of the Kingdom and to live from a heavenly position. This cost our Heavenly Father the life of His only

Son. It was Jesus' sacrifice on the cross that paid the *full* price for our sin so we can ultimately have intimacy with the Godhead and walk in our inheritance of freedom and authority.

What is the Father asking you?

Invite Jesus to open up His love letter—the Bible—to you and call you into a deeper life of surrender to Him.

Spend your life for the King; obedience is always better than sacrifice. The passage ends with, *"He called on the Lord, and the Lord answered him with fire from heaven on the altar of burnt offering."* (1 Chronicles 21:26-b.)

David honored God, and David's sacrifice was honored by the Lord; the plague was stopped, the angel put away his sword, David got his answer from the Lord, and later the threshing floor became the site for the temple.

God honors our sacrifices. Are you willing to pay the full price and go all in with Jesus?

DEEP CALLS
TO DEEP

*And my speech and my preaching were not with persuasive words of human wisdom,
but in demonstration of the Spirit and of power, that your faith should not be in the
wisdom of men but in the power of God.*
1 Corinthians 2:4-6 NKJ

Where are diamonds, rubies, and sapphires found? They don't lie scattered on top of the ground where anyone can casually pick them up and do whatever they want with them. These precious stones lie hidden deep within the earth. It's the same way in the spiritual realm.

The wisdom and direction you need and the gifts God has given you are hidden deep down inside of you, like precious treasures waiting to be discovered. But you have to be ready to receive these treasures.

How do you get ready?

The answer is through daily times of intimate fellowship with God. *"Those that hunger and thirst for righteousness shall be filled."* (Matthew 5:6.) He *always* feeds the hungry souls. When the deep in us calls to deep in God, when His waves and His breakers wash over us, it creates a cry for hunger and thirst that pulls us into the depths of His treasures.

As a scuba diver prepares to explore the vast, deep ocean, he readies himself with the proper equipment, and takes great care to ensure that he knows how to navigate the waters. Similarly, we can venture deep down to find treasures and rarities that our Heavenly Father has made available for us.

Keep diving.

Keep seeking.

Keep knocking.

Keep stirring up hunger, and keep thirsting for living water. Press on and find the treasures that are deep within you: the rubies, the diamonds, the rarities, and the beautiful life that lies hidden in the deep waters of your spirit.

Our life is hidden in Christ.

You are a unique and precious treasure; you are a rare find. There are beauties to be discovered in you, to be heard through you, and to be seen through you.

I encourage you to meditate on the following scriptures. The deep places within you will rise up as you seek to know the deep places in God:

1 Corinthians 2:4-10 - Deep calls to deep, continued.

Psalm 42:7 - Deep calls to deep in the roar of your waterfalls; all your waves and breakers have swept over me.

Psalm 42:1 - As a deer pants for streams of water, so my soul pants for you, O God. My soul thirsts for God, for the living God. Where can I go and meet with God? My tears have been my food all night, while men say to me all day long, "Where is your God?"

Matthew 5:6 - Jesus said: "Blessed are those that hunger and thirst for righteousness for they shall be filled."

Isaiah 55:3 - Incline your ear and come to Me; listen, so that your soul may live. I will make an everlasting covenant with you, my faithful love promised to David.

Psalm 63:2 - I have seen you in the sanctuary and beheld your power and glory.

Psalm 47:7 - For God is the King of all the earth; sing praises with understanding.

FILL YOUR HORN
WITH OIL AND GO

The Lord said to Samuel, "How long will you mourn for Saul since I have rejected him as King over Israel? Fill your horn with oil and be on your way; I am sending you to Jesse of Bethlehem. I have chosen one of his sons to be King." But Samuel said, "How can I go? If Saul hears about it, he will kill me." The Lord said, "Take a heifer with you and say, 'I have come to sacrifice to the Lord.' Invite Jesse to the sacrifice, and I will show you what to do. You are to anoint for Me the one I indicate.

1 Samuel 16:1-3 NIV

What is a Horn? It is a symbol of Authority, Victory, Strength, and Grace. What is Oil? It is a symbol for the anointing of God. Oil represents the Holy Spirit in the Old Testament. In this case, it is consecrated and sacred. The anointing oil was sprinkled on or poured on the heads of those set apart for service and to carry out assignments. The anointing was an act of dedication and consecration.

In reference to the scripture above, Israel needed a new and better leader, but David first needed to be anointed. We need to fill our earthen vessel with the Oil of the Holy Spirit and do what God has assigned us to do under His anointing.

When Saul was anointed King, a man-made flask was used to pour out the oil. But when David was anointed, an animal's horn was used, signifying that blood was shed. When the horn was cut from the animal, blood was shed. The blood of Jesus' sacrifice on the cross had to happen before the Holy Spirit could come and Pentecost could happen (Acts 2).

Without Oil, there is no anointing. God wanted Samuel to fill his horn with oil and anoint David as king.

As God required Samuel to fill his horn with oil, He also requires us to fill ourselves with Him. We must make a daily choice to do this; to surrender what is ruling our heart, that God has rejected. Saul was rejected, but he didn't know it. He was still on the throne, but the anointing had lifted.

In our own lives, we tend to believe that our past has authority and a voice of rulership. Let us have the courage of Samuel.

The Lord said, *"Samuel, stop mourning. I have rejected your past!"* There is always a price to be paid for the sacrifices we make as we walk toward the life that we are called into by Jesus. God will have us, through His blood, fill our horn with the Oil of the Holy Spirit, pour it out, and rule from a new place. A full horn is more difficult to crush than an empty horn. *"I am pressed but not crushed...persecuted but not abandoned."* (2 Corinthians 4:8.)

Is your horn full of Oil or empty?

You can keep talking about the hurt or talk about God's goodness. You can keep asking why or hold fast to the hope laid before you.

The time to get more Oil is now!

No longer can we wait and get by on the faith of those who came before us. It's time to fill up our horn and go. Go into your future, into your destiny.

Leave your past behind and go. Stop allowing what God has rejected to control your emotions. Imagine what would have happened if Samuel hadn't gone out again; David would not have taken his place as Israel's greatest King.

As you walk through this week, allow the Holy Spirit to pour out from a fresh new place. Behold I am doing a new thing, winter is gone, and springtime has come! Hunger brings you the fresh Oil, the sacred Oil, and puts a "go" in your spirit that you can't deny.

So, this week go in the strength of the Lord, and go in the power of His might!

INTERSECTIONS

Does not wisdom cry out, and understanding lift up her voice?
She takes her stand on the top of the high hill, beside the way where the paths meet.
Proverbs 8:1-2 NKJ

❝ Slow down, you're going too fast! Do we turn left? Do we turn right? Is there a roundabout?"

Every day we are presented with intersections. Where is God taking us? What is the direction He is leading us by the Spirit of the Lord? Proverbs often speaks of intersections, crossroads, pathways, all similar definitions of the way the Father leads us.

What is crying out at your intersection in the busyness of your life? In the noisy places at the city gates?

So many voices. Who are you listening to?

I love the Book of Proverbs because it leads us to the instruction of wisdom. Both Proverbs 1 and Proverbs 8 talk about wisdom and how it cries out in the intersections. James 1:5 says: *"When we lack wisdom, we can freely ask, and God will give it to us."* We can come boldly to the throne of grace and receive the mercy that's needed and is new every morning. In the time and the hour that we are living in, wisdom is crying out in many of our intersections, crossroads, and pathways of life, family, finances, ministry, jobs, and children.

Cry out to the Lord and then incline your ear to the instruction of wisdom. God will freely give what you ask for.

Keep asking.

Keep knocking.

Keep seeking.

God is the Beginning and the End. He's in the leaning. He's in the quiet secret place. *"Trust in the Lord, and don't lean on your own understanding."* (Proverbs 3:5). *"Guard your heart."* (Proverbs 4:23). *"Acknowledge Him in all of your ways, and He will make your path straight."* (Proverbs 3:6).

Paths that lead to righteousness, paths that were once crooked will become straight. Valleys that were low will become high. Cry aloud for wisdom in the intersections of your day.

Let God lead you by still waters and give you peace that surpasses your understanding. God's wisdom will guard your heart and your mind in Christ Jesus, the Lover of your soul.

I encourage you to read and meditate on Proverbs chapter 1 and chapter 8, and let the Lord speak to your heart.

NO FLOATIES

Then we will no longer be like babies. We will not be people who are always changing like a ship that the waves carry one way and then another. We will not be influenced by every new teaching we hear from people who are trying to deceive us–those who make clever plans and use every of trick to fool others into following the wrong way.
Ephesians 4:14 ERV

I went to a beautiful restaurant for dinner one evening. The waiter poured a tall, crystal glass full of water for me. As I reached for the glass to take a drink, I noticed something was in my water. It was tiny and it was swimming! I had a full glass of water, but there was one little thing that caused me not to want the entire glass.

In God, there is no mixture. Revelation 22:1 says, *"Then the angel showed me the river of the water of life, as clear as crystal, flowing from the throne of God."* This crystal-clear river of life flowing from God's throne is the Zoe life of God. It is the life of God given to us through Jesus.

What does devotion in this day and hour look like? What does love one-another in this hour and time look like? How do we honor each other above ourselves with genuine affection? Have you noticed that there are a lot of questionable things vying for our attention, trying to steal our devotion?

As we set our thoughts, our minds, and our devotion on Him, His thoughts will become our thoughts, and His ways will become our ways. This produces an unadulterated life, one without dilution or mixture, that comes from the Zoe life of God.

How do we live an unadulterated life?

It comes from a deep hunger for the pure life of God. In the same way that one recognizes a counterfeit twenty-dollar bill; by being intimately acquainted with the real thing. It's then that a counterfeit can be identified by its feel and appearance. Ephesians 4:14 warns us about the winds of false doctrine by the craftiness of men coming from every angle.

In this hour, it is essential that we spend time with the authentic, true, pure, and real God. Then, as we are faced with counterfeit theology, distractions or temptations, we will not be moved by every new teaching that comes our way.

The wind moves and we do not see it, but we will see the effects of the wind. May God make us so sensitive that when the wind blows, we will not be moved. We will know the true wind of the Spirit versus the wind of false doctrine as we become more in line with the Word of God.

I challenge you to go after God's heart. Live a life that is so full of the presence of God that there isn't room for mixture with worldly things. There is no greater honor than to experience God's presence.

Where might there be a mixture in your life? Are there things limiting you? Ask the Lord for a great desire and a deep hunger for an uncompromised, unadulterated relationship with Jesus. Seek Him, and He will be found. He will always feed your hungry heart. He is ravenous for you. Nothing else, just you and *all* of your heart.

THE STRETCH
OF FAITH

Make your tent bigger. Open your doors wide. Don't think small!
Make your tent large and strong, because you will grow in all directions.
Your children will take over many nations and live in the cities that were destroyed.
Don't be afraid! You will not be disappointed.
People will not say bad things against you. You will not be embarrassed.
When you were young, you felt shame. But you will forget that shame.
You will not remember the shame you felt when you lost your husband.
Isaiah 54:1-4 ERV

This scripture defines an act of faith.

But, what is an *act?* An act means to take action; do something, as in "caught in the act."

What is *faith?* Faith is a belief and trust in the loyalty of God. Hebrews 11:1 says: *"Faith is the substance of things hoped for and the evidence of things not seen."*

We cannot live small.

I was praying one morning for the Sanctioned Love team, and the increase of our vision for the ministry.

I heard in my heart from the Lord, *"Thank you for being willing to say yes to the stretch and allow the stretch marks to be seen on your life."*

Acts of faith causes the mark of the stretch on our life.

I then had understanding in my heart for what came next from the Lord. He said, *"Never go into a covenant relationship with people who do not appreciate the stretch marks on your life. I have allowed those marks on your life to show the price of the seed you have carried."*

When we walk in what God has for us, there is a stretch that can leave a mark on our lives. Faith is always in the unseen acts of doing and standing.

Acts of faith cause the mark of stretch on your life.

Others will not like the stretch marks on your life. People want everything to be airbrushed and quick. However; to carry a seed in a womb and for that seed to grow, it takes time and will stretch you.

You are about to birth something, a passion. Allow the pain and tenderness of the stretch to not look pretty for a while, so the seed of passion from the Lord can be birthed through you. Those who appreciate the stretch marks will see the seed turn into fruit in, and on your life.

WHAT IS IN YOUR HAND?

And the Lord said to Moses, "Cut two tablets of stone like the first ones, and I will
write on these tablets the words that were on the first tablets which you broke.
So be ready in the morning, and come up in the morning to Mount Sinai,
and present yourself to Me there on the top of the mountain.
And no man shall come up with you, and let no man be seen throughout the
mountain; let neither flocks nor herds feed before that mountain.
Exodus 34:1-3 NKJ

H ave you ever felt discouraged?
Have you ever felt like the very thing the Lord has placed in your heart, a passion or desire that you have been holding onto for a very long time, is slipping away?

One morning, I was reading and praying, asking the Lord about a heavy place regarding a heart-desire in my life. The Lord led me to Exodus.

Moses had gone up for forty days and forty nights onto Mt. Sinai to be in the glory and the presence of God, and there He spoke to Moses from the cloud. He gave Moses two tablets of testimony, written on tablets of stone. God cut the tablets out of rock and wrote on them with His finger. The Lord placed these in Moses' hands to deliver to the people. Due to the fact that Moses was delayed coming down the mountain, the Israelites started indulging in their own fleshly desires, and worshiping idols, and false gods. As Moses came back down, he heard the Israelites singing. Exodus 32:19 says, *"So it was as soon as he came near the camp that he saw the calf and the people dancing. So, Moses' anger became hot, and he cast the tablets out of his hands and broke them at the foot of the mountain."*

Have you ever noticed that the Lord didn't really get mad at the Israelites? He had Moses come back up the mountain and back into His presence. Moses had to cut the rock himself the second time, but God still wrote with His finger the instructions on the tablets.

When Moses looked at what people were doing around him, he lost his hold on the very thing that God had placed in his hand. This was difficult for me to hear because I felt like the Lord was strongly encouraging me not to lose my hold on what He had written on my heart.

What has God asked you to carry? What has He written on the scroll of your life? Don't be distracted by what people around you are saying or doing, or your circumstances.

Be encouraged.

Stay in His presence.

"Look up from where your help always comes from." (Psalm 121:1-2.) *"His mercy is new every morning."* (Lamentations 3:22-23), and *"His grace is sufficient."* (2 Corinthians 12:9.) *"We walk by faith and not by sight."* (2 Corinthians 5:7.)

Speak to the circumstances and hold fast to the promises that are in your hand.

GUESS WHO'S COMING TO DINNER?

Co-authored and edited by Nicole Boyd

The table is set with the finest china you own. Candles have been lit and the centerpiece flowers you worked three hours on look fabulous. The seven-course meal you planned has taken nearly three days of preparation. You look around the dining room one last time, straighten the silverware, stand back, and sigh. Yep, everything looks perfect.

A knock sounds at the door and you quickly take off your apron, straighten your hair and check your makeup in the mirror in the hall. You take one last look around your home. It's never been so clean. And it's only right that it should be. When God is coming to dinner, you must present your very best.

You take a deep breath and open the door. Father God is standing on your doorstep. He smiles, "Hello, sweetheart. May I come in?"

"Of course!" you exclaim, and open the door wide. You lead Him into the dining room and He seems impressed. You offer Him a seat but He declines. He instead pulls out the chair for you.

"I don't understand?" you say, as you reluctantly sit down and He scoots the chair in for you.

He smiles and says, "Tonight, I serve you."

You look up at Him, dumbfounded. This was not how you had envisioned the evening going. This isn't right. *You* should be serving Him, not the other way around. Right?

A lot of times in our Christian walk we treat God as the guest of honor at the table. We take great pains to set the table of our lives to impress Him. We clean house (as best we can) before we invite Him into our home. Guests do not prepare the dinner. Guests do not help with washing dishes. And guests are only allowed in the special rooms of the house. They are most definitely not shown the "catch-all room" on the tour. You know, the room where you tossed all the toys and dirty clothes that had been sitting around before your guest arrived?

But the fact of the matter is, Father God is not the guest; He is the host. God has paid the ultimate price to adopt us into His family. He is the one who has prepared a seven-course meal for us and invited us to His table. He does the dishes, and then He goes into the rooms of our hearts that we allow Him into to clean up the dirty socks and crusty pizza boxes.

But why is it so hard to see Him doing the dirty work? Perhaps it's because in every other religion, the false gods demand to be served their every (evil) whim at the expense of their followers.

My team and I recently went on a trip to India, and I was shocked by the living conditions. Everywhere we went, people were living in squalor, trying to scrape by as best they could while their temples were covered in gold and lavish meals laid out for the gods. But their gods do not answer them. I was so honored to share the love of the only one and true God. The God who always feeds the hungry and heals the brokenhearted. The God who takes off His outer garment, wraps a towel around His waist, and washes our feet.

Christianity is the only religion where our God sets a table before us and our needs are provided for. Our God is a good Father, the best Father, who values relationship. He is a Father who gives good gifts to his children.

So, what are these gifts? How do we use them? The truth is, many of us have been given gifts that we have refused to open. Thoughts like, "I don't deserve this. I'm scared of what's in the box. I'm not sure if that is for today," are holding us back from opening the amazing gifts that God has given to us. And the fact is that these gifts are not just for you! They're to share our amazing Father's love with those around us.

How would you feel as a child on Christmas, if your brother or sister had a present that was for you and your siblings, and they didn't want to open and share it with you?

Come to the bounty of the Father's table, where the lost are always found, the thirsty are quenched, and the hungry are always fed.

The question is, are you hungry?

Bon appetite!

HANNAH DAVENPORT

There's a common misconception that people believe when they're saved, they will never have to experience hard times. That certainly wasn't the case for me.

I practically grew up in church and accepted Christ at a very young age. He has always been a constant companion and presence in my life, and I chose Jesus over everything.

Shortly into my teenage years, my relationship with the Holy Spirit got deeper. I turned to Him for the answers to everything and, as a result, I assumed life would be carefree. That is, until the devil came straight for me with what most teens struggle with all the time: identity.

As the devil whispered in my ear, I struggled with knowing who I really was for a couple of years.

Everything started to change during my sophomore year of high school. I was tired of believing the lies of the enemy and I knew something needed to change. Whenever those lies began to creep into my thoughts, I found the verses of truth and spoke them over myself.

Our words are mighty. They can either bring life or death, and I wanted to live.

I started to see freedom in my life, and I couldn't stay quiet. By the time I had graduated from high school, I knew the truth and I believed it with all my heart. I went directly into youth leadership and I recognized my former situation and internal battles within my students. I knew exactly what they were struggling with and I wanted them to see their true identity.

Through my journey, I've had the opportunity to spread the message of our Heavenly Father about our identity in Christ and that we should never replace it with what others say about us. Sharing my story about discovering my identity has not only changed my life, but the lives of many teens who have gone through the same thing.

Just know you are never alone in this thing called life; the Lord is right there with you, fighting your battles.

IDENTITY

I will give thanks and praise You, for I am fearfully and wonderfully made;
wonderful are Your works, and my soul knows it very well.
Psalm 139:14 AMP

I t all started with a look from another girl in the eighth grade. I'd seen her around the school over the last few years, but something was different about her this year. She was one of the popular girls, and I was definitely, well, not. The look she gave me that day was one that I'll never forget because of the way it made me feel. The way her expression said, *"You're different,"* and *"you'll never be one of us."* Or, as the devil wanted me to believe, her look said,

"You.

Don't.

Matter."

I was someone who kept to myself. I didn't have many friends. On top of that, I'd never had a boyfriend. It was at this point in time when my identity and self-image began to break down and my insecurities consumed me. Rumors began to circulate around school that I was a lesbian because I didn't date, but that was the furthest thing from the truth. I began to believe the lie that I wasn't pretty, and I couldn't be as desirable as some of the other girls.

When you listen to those lies long enough, you eventually start to believe them. The lies begin to attach themselves to your identity, and that's exactly what happened to me.

I grew up in the church, so I had heard it a million times before; that you should "never put your identity or worth into anyone but Jesus because we are made in His image." But what I had done was compare myself to others and what they thought of me. Inspirational speaker and coach, Abi Stumvoll, quoted, *"If we compare ourselves to the perfection in our head or what others think of us, we can begin to destroy ourselves."* Never has there been a truer statement.

From that first day in the eighth grade, that's exactly what I started to do. I believed for so long that what other people thought of me was more important than what God thought of me. I began to destroy myself from the inside out. My constant comparison was like a cancer eating away at my self-worth. I was not loving myself or seeing myself the way Jesus saw me.

Never put your identity or worth into anyone but Jesus because we are made in His image.

Mark 12: 30 – 31 says: *"Love the Lord your God with all your heart and with all your soul and with all your mind and with all your strength.... Love your neighbor as yourself...There are no commandments greater than these."*

So many people who have identity issues have this belief that they are not worthy of being loved. For me, identity always goes back to this verse: *"This is the kind of love we are talking about—not that we once upon a time loved God, but that He loved us and sent His Son as a sacrifice to clear away our sins and the damage they've done to our relationship with God."* 1 John 4:10.

The truth is, we don't deserve love simply because we're so awesome on the inside or beautiful on the outside. We are worthy of love because of what He has done for us. It's not prideful to think of ourselves in a positive light because our worth doesn't come from our own power, it comes from Jesus.

If we are not careful, we can get ourselves stuck in what I like to call the Shame Cycle, which can sometimes make it seem like you'll never make it out until you truly know your identity in Christ.

I feel unworthy

I feel ashamed

so then I hide

Then I feel disconnected

when I feel disconnected...

It wasn't until a couple of years later that things started to turn around for me. I was sitting in youth group, and my youth pastor was preaching on Psalm 139:14, which says, *"I will give thanks and praise to You, for I am fearfully and wonderfully made; Wonderful are Your works, and my soul knows it very well."* I had spent so many years placing my identity in the opinions of other people. I realized that night, that the only person's opinion I had to concern myself with was God's. That night revolutionized how I saw myself. I began to speak this verse over myself anytime I would feel those lies try to creep their way back into my life.

So how do you get freedom and overcome your identity issues? Find someone to talk about your struggles with, speak Scriptures over yourself, and begin to listen to what Father God says about you, instead of what others think of you.

My identity struggles were silenced with the verse in Jeremiah 1:5a: *"Before I formed you in the womb I knew you, before you were born, I set you apart."* Trust in these words, and speak them over yourself when you're feeling unworthy.

We are all loved by our Heavenly Father, and if you ever need a reminder, speak the verse of Genesis 1:27: *"So God created mankind in His own image, in the image of God, He created them; male and female He created them."* God has done some amazing work, and He created us with all of His love. We are truly special and unique, and that in itself is a gift.

I often spoke the verse, 1 Peter 2:9 over myself, *"But you are a chosen people, a royal priesthood, a holy nation, God's special possession, that you may declare the praises of Him who called you out of darkness into His wonderful light. "* These words carry a commanding and unspoken need for self-acceptance. It goes without saying that we have been chosen by God to live this life, and we must see and love ourselves as He does in order to bring honor to the Holy Spirit.

A negative body image is a common problem among all people, young and old. We are constantly changing, growing, evolving into ourselves, and in the troubled times that we look in the mirror and don't like what we see, remember that we are created in His image. Love yourself! *"Do you not know that your bodies are temples of the Holy Spirit, who is in you, whom you have received from God? You are not your own; you were bought at a price. Therefore, honor God with your bodies. "* (1 Corinthians 6:19-20).

You are beautiful, just the way you are.

NATALIE DAVENPORT

As part of Sanctioned Love Ministry, my piece of the puzzle is to lead people into the presence of God through worship. Worship has been my main communion with God and it has brought me out of some tough and challenging situations throughout my life. My writings for this book have come from a journey that had left me quite broken, and only Jesus has been able to pick up my shattered pieces and put me back together again.

I've struggled with anxiety and depression since I was a young child. I've had great difficulty in relationships. I've never felt understood, and I felt isolated and alone through most of my childhood and teenage years. Over the last decade, I have walked over high hills and through low valleys, but I had seemed to be stuck in those low valleys. After taking a look at my own heart, I realized there were many coping mechanisms—fear, distrust, and control issues—that were holding me back from living the best life God had for me. These last few years have been my most difficult season, but I have seen the most growth in letting go and letting God heal the broken pieces of my life. There has been a great need for vulnerability and honesty with those who I've built deep trust with.

But through it all, there has been so much beauty in the mess. I'm learning that I have the choice to let God in, to let Him shed light on the darkest of situations, and pull me up into the calling He has on my life. I am forever grateful for the constant love of God, for He has never failed me, and He never will.

ARDENT
WORSHIPERS

Yet a time is coming and has now come when the true worshipers will worship the
Father in the Spirit and in truth, for they are the kind of worshipers the Father seeks. God
is Spirit, and His worshipers must worship in the Spirit and in truth.
John 4:23-24 NIV

Ardent: Adjective - enthusiastic or passionate.

Synonyms: avid, fervent, wholehearted, intense, and fierce.

Worship is more than a song; it is a lifestyle.
When we live a life of worship, every fiber of our being cries out in adoration to the Creator of the universe. We should be so passionate about our walk with the Lord. Every waking moment should be to glorify His name.

I want to be a wholehearted worshiper.

I want to be an *ardent worshiper.*

I want my life to sing of the faithfulness of God, to ring out the promises of a Holy God.

Wouldn't you agree that living a life of ardent worship isn't always our fleshly desire? We can get caught up in the day-to-day tasks and live only to survive. We go from worship service to worship service, looking for the next best outpouring of the Holy Spirit when we can simply access the Spirit in our personal lives of worship.

The Holy Spirit lives inside us and enables us to commune with Father God anytime, anywhere. This reality puts a fire in my heart to worship the King of Kings and the Lord of Lords. God's great sacrifice of Jesus allows me to walk in an intimate relationship with Him. Therefore, why wouldn't I give my all during worship? Why wouldn't I be enthusiastic and passionate in my worship?

My life, how I live day-to-day, should express that enthusiasm for the life-giving blood of Jesus' sacrifice. Romans 12:1-2 describes how our lives should be living sacrifices, and this is a way that we worship God. *"Therefore, I urge you, brothers and sisters, in view of God's mercy, to offer your bodies as a living sacrifice, holy and pleasing to God—this is your true and proper worship. Do not conform to the pattern of this world, but be transformed by the renewing of your mind. Then you will be able to test and approve what God's will is—His good, pleasing, and perfect will."*

Let us always take time to honor God in our lives and not take for granted the awe-inspiring work that Jesus accomplished on the cross. May we never take for granted the access of God's presence and His never-ending longing to commune with His sons and daughters.

How can you become an ardent worshiper? It's easy! Take some time to study the scriptures and read about what God has to say about worship. Set aside thirty minutes each week to turn on some worship music, or play an instrument, and create your own worship time.

Let God encounter you with His love and joy. Then, grab your journal and write about what you think it means to be an ardent worshiper.

NOTHING HIDDEN

If your heart is broken, you'll find God right there;
if you're kicked in the gut, He'll help you catch your breath.
Psalm 34:18 MSG

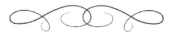

This is my pain, deep down inside.
It's hidden in crevices for no one to find.
It comes with unwanted shame and self-doubt.
A pride that says I'll be unwanted if someone finds out.
This ugly hidden life that's been a coping mechanism
Is starting to eat away at the joy that I've been given.
There comes a point in the road where I have to make a decision.
Am I going to let Jesus in the middle or keep it hidden?
Even though I understand that God sees it all,
It's natural to feel that I've gone too far,
From the grace that God freely gives when I fall.
As much as it hurts to verbalize,
There's a fork in the road, and I realize
I have to overcome the fear of rejection
To find my freedom and regain my connection.
So, I invite You, God, into this moment,
where I feel so completely broken.
I give You my shame and my darkest secrets.
I want to live life with nothing hidden.

—*Natalie Davenport*

Sometimes we struggle to deal with the struggle. One thing we, the sons and daughters of God, need to realize is that God is not afraid of our emotions. He's not afraid of our messes. He's waiting for us to run to Him with all our brokenness and pain, so He can heal our hearts as only He can.

Take the time to ask Jesus to come into those parts of your life that seem icky and undesirable. Let Him release His unconditional love into your place of shame and hurt. Only He can mend a broken heart and restore your joy and your hope.

SEAL THE DEAL

Therefore, I tell you, whatever you ask for in prayer,
believe that you have received it, and it will be yours.
Mark 11:24 NIV

For most of you reading this, I think it would be safe to say that there are things you have been praying for, and it's been a long journey of keeping the faith. Holding onto the promises of God is most certainly not a walk in the park. On this day, I want to offer encouragement for you to keep holding on to those promises and to reignite the faith that spurred you on this great journey to believe in God's miraculous power.

Like some of you reading this, I, too, have struggled with believing and hoping for the promises of God to come to pass. I've cried out to God for many things in my life. Many of these prayers include my future husband and our future children, because frankly, sometimes I feel like I'm going to be single forever. I've had dreams and visions for my life of travel and leading worship that I have been fervently praying for since I was a little girl. I've been believing for healing in my body and have yet to see the completed healing. I do not say this to bring discredit to God because I know He sees my heart and desires to see the miracles in my own life. I know His plans are to prosper me and

His plans are to prosper me and bring about His goodness in my life.

bring about His goodness in my life. It will all come to pass in His timing.

As I've journeyed through this season of promises unfulfilled, I had started to doubt and let discouragement take root in my own heart. I had questioned whether God was going to come through for me. I began to let my dreams fall to the wayside, and I had become apathetic. I had settled for second best in my heart. I used to think to myself, *maybe life would be better if I was a bachelorette my whole life. Maybe I don't even want children.* And, sometimes I'd think, *I'll learn to live with chronic pain and cope with life.*

Then, my whole perception changed after a brief phone call with my mother. We were having a conversation about my faith for my physical healing, and she posed the question, "How do we need to be praying for you? Are you still believing for your healing, or have you grown weary?" My response to my mother broke my own heart. I responded and heard the emptiness in my words, "I don't have any faith right now to pray for myself. I'm struggling to believe that God is going to heal me, but I'm thankful that you can stand in the gap for me." At that moment, I realized that I had given up, and I had to find a way back to a place of faith in God's power to heal me. I needed my hope to be restored and my fire to be reignited.

A week or so later, I was standing in my kitchen talking to God about my present situation. My heart was laid bare before Him, ready for Him to speak and give direction. I knew that God was already aware of the hurt in my heart and the pain I was going through, but I wanted to be vulnerable with God and verbalize my feelings to Him. I told Him about my anger and how I had given up on my healing. He gently spoke to my heart and said, "*Natalie, when you begin to believe that I, God, cannot fulfill the promises that I have made to you, you deny the very power of what Jesus did for you on the cross.*" God has a way of bringing discipline and correction that is not judgmental, but it opens our eyes to our wrong perceptions of who He is.

What a wakeup call that brief moment was!

I repented of my wrong thinking and asked God to give me hope and steadfastness to believe for my healing, to believe that He was going to be faithful in bringing me my future husband and give me those precious babies. He is completing a good work in me, and He is going to bring those promises to pass. In my vulnerability and honesty with God, He *is* going to hear my heart's cry and move with compassion in my situation. I believe it with all of my heart that healing is coming, my husband is coming, and my babies are coming. No disease, or yet-to-be-fulfilled desire of my heart is going to squelch the faith I have in a God who knows and sees every little detail of my life.

WHEN LIFE GIVES YOU LEMONS... WORSHIP!

At this, Job got up and tore his robe and shaved his head. Then he fell to the ground in worship and said: 'Naked I came from my mother's womb, and naked I will depart. The Lord gave, and the Lord has taken away; may the name of the Lord be praised'. In all this, Job did not sin by charging God with wrongdoing.
Job 1:20-22 NIV

If only worshiping through the hardest times of life was as easy as Job makes it out to be. This man of God lost everything that meant anything to him in his life, yet he still praised God.

Life is going to give us lemons, but what kind of lemonade are we going to make? Will it be sour: displeasing to God and our fellow man? Or will it be sweet: holy and acceptable to the Lord and a testimony of God's faithfulness to those lives we affect?

I remember a time recently in my life that I questioned why God would let bad things happen to good people. I was diagnosed with endometriosis in 2018, and I live in a constant state of varying degrees of pain. When I first started showing symptoms in the summer of 2017, they were bad enough to warrant multiple appointments with my physician. I questioned—quite verbally—to God, what in the world was I doing wrong to deserve this? I've always believed that God heals, but my healing wasn't coming. I was depressed, angry, worn out, and I felt secluded in my problems. In those moments of frustration, I had to make a choice, and quick! I could choose to jump on the pity party train, or I could choose to worship. The most amazing thing I have seen God do through this whole ordeal is that, not once, has God *not* been present when I needed Him. He has always sent the Holy Spirit to bring comfort to my heart. He has surrounded me with family and close friends to continually keep me lifted up in prayer.

Maybe I haven't seen my complete healing yet, but I choose to believe that God is good. I choose to worship when life is throwing me lemons. My problems are never going to keep me from my ministry of worship. And you know what? Every time I get behind my piano to worship, I somehow forget about my symptoms, and I can focus on worshipping the King of Kings and the Lord of Lords.

So, which are you going to choose? Choose today to make the sweetest, most delectable glass of lemonade and let your life speak of the faithfulness and goodness of God.

SANDIE DOUGHTY

How do you write a testimony of your life, describing the exact moment when Jesus interrupted everything?

Jesus was always in the back of my mind as I grew up. I was raised to believe in Jesus, and my earliest memories of Him are centered around church. I learned that He loves and forgives, but I don't remember learning much else.

When I was a freshman in high school, my parents divorced. I never went to church again. After that, my life started to change. I chose to taste the wild side of life—parties and drugs. I ended up getting married and then divorced. I practiced wild and crazy living to the best of my ability, chasing after anything I thought would fill the void in my heart. It only left me lonely and empty. I eventually ended up in Mexico with my boyfriend. That's when things really started to crumble. My boyfriend's family was very dysfunctional; the environment we were in consisted of violent fistfights, dangerous situations, and at one point, a policeman taunted me with a gun. It was a stark contrast to the calm and quiet that I was used to.

While traveling through Mexico, we were robbed at gunpoint. They took everything, and then they let us go. Life was happening to me without my consent and it took its toll. My last night in Mexico was spent pinned to the wall and being threatened by a jealous boyfriend. I had wanted to leave for some time, but my boyfriend's family didn't believe my stories until one of his brothers saw this situation in action. Finally, that was it; I was given money to go home.

I returned to my hometown, broken and disillusioned.

Shortly after, my sister invited me to a "Jesus event." I decided that I would go, just to observe. While I was there I felt the Holy Spirit's presence. It was as if He were pursuing me.

Then, one day in my mom's living room, I felt it. With the sun shining in through the windows, I "tapped out." I gave up, gave in, and I surrendered to Jesus. In a split-second, my thoughts about life, my emotions, all the empty, lonely, and broken places of my heart changed. My heart became whole and full; my thoughts were filled with thankfulness. Jesus took up residence in my heart. For some beautiful reason, when you "tap out" with Jesus, you feel like you have won the match. The surrender becomes the victory. Now I call Him my King, my best friend, my soulmate.

This is the heart that I write from.

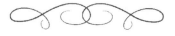

Don't Let the Enemy Put You into His Jail

And do not be conformed to this world, but be transformed by the renewing of your mind, that you may prove what is good and acceptable and perfect will of God.
Romans 12:2 NKJ

As I was worshiping this morning, I discovered something profound; I had been taking counsel from "fear." We may not think of fear as actually having a voice in our thought process because it has become such a familiar presence. It can affect our thoughts about ourselves, friendships or circumstances in our lives.

I realized that in certain areas of my life fear was keeping me locked up, or in jail.

Let me explain.

These fearful thoughts can become permanent highways, like well-worn paths inside our minds which can become a personal bondage, or jail cell. These are thoughts that are not in alignment with God's Word. As Christians, our lives, our thoughts and the intentions of our hearts are always being discipled by our teacher, the Holy Spirit. John 14:26 says: *"But the Helper, the Holy Spirit, whom the Father will send in My name, He will teach you all things and bring to remembrance all that I said to you."* If we decide not to listen, we can fall back into old fearful patterns again.

Addiction, fear, competition, insecurities; Jesus doesn't want any of those things mastering us. He wants us to master them. If they control us, then they hold the key to the jail cell in our minds.

Some of us feel as though we are imprisoned and we want to get out of these patterns, but we just end up back in jail while someone else holds the key. Why? Because, as Genesis 4:7 says: *"...sin is lying in wait for you, ready to pounce, it's out to get you, you've got to master it!"*

As Christians, our lives, our thoughts, and the intentions of our hearts are always being discipled by our teacher, the Holy Spirit.

Repeated over and over again, negative, fearful thinking sours our souls and causes us to feel bitter, helpless, and most often lacking peace. Eventually, we find ourselves, once again, taking council from our fears. When we accept these thought patterns, they dominate us because we failed to trust God and Holy Spirit to lead us.

Fail is a strong word, but it is not a word that scares our God. His compassion and mercy for you is brand new every day. Lamentations 3:22-24 says: *"God's loyal love couldn't have run out; His merciful love couldn't have dried up. They are created new every morning. How great is your faithfulness!"*

Failure is a word that the enemy of our soul loves to use. The enemy uses repeated negative thought patterns, hoping we don't recognize the untruths. No one wants to stay in jail, with repeated thought patterns; we want to find a better way. We want to overcome and **have success.**

When we choose to surrender and trust the Holy Spirit to show us a better way, we will have freedom. As a Jesus-believer, I call it dying to my own wisdom, and my own ways, and being willing to trust God and His ways.

Christ uses this example in His Word. John 12:24 says*: "I tell you the truth unless a kernel of wheat is planted in the soil and dies, it remains only a single seed, but if it dies, it's death will produce many seeds, a plentiful harvest!"* A harvest of freedom! We must trust the process in Christ, so we can look forward to a plentiful harvest!

Someone once told me the acronym for FEAR:

False

Evidence

Appearing

Real.

I think of this often when I notice I am offended, fearful, or assuming. The enemy likes to stack up false evidence so that we start to believe his lies, and...

We end up in jail again.

Practice renewing your mind by reading His Word. Romans12:2 says: *"Do not be conformed to the pattern of this world but be transformed by the renewing of your mind. Then you will be able to test and approve what God's will is, His good, pleasing and perfect will."*

We learn wisdom, understanding, and counsel from reading His Word.

When we are partaking of something that goes against His wisdom, a scripture will pop up into our minds. At that moment, we have an opportunity to choose which way we want to go in this intersection of our thoughts. If you choose the wisdom out of His Word, repeatedly, you will build up your spiritual muscles. If you decide to keep believing the false accusations and entertain them, you are exercising your fleshly muscles, and there you go, back into jail.

God tells us we have been given a sound mind, power, and love, which all come from our relationship with Him, by reading His Word, by worshipping Him, and hanging out with Him. We were not given a spirit of fear.

If you are reading this but have not decided whether you want to accept Christ into your heart, know this: the wisdom in His Word, the Bible, is an excellent guide for you to walk away from fear and into freedom.

Meditate on scriptures and continue to develop your spiritual muscles. You will soon recognize the difference between the enemy's deception and lies, and when our Heavenly Father is giving you wisdom and the key to get out of jail.

Welcome to freedom!

ENTER INTO HIS GATES WITH THANKSGIVING

Enter into His courts with thanksgiving, and into His gates with praise.
Be thankful to Him and bless His name.
Psalm 100:4 NKJ

Great is Thy faithfulness.

I'm thankful, Lord, that you created an avenue of praise and worship. An avenue whose street sign reads "Thanksgiving." When we find thanksgiving, we enter into His house and His gates.

I *need* to have that avenue of praise and worship.

Pressing in and declaring who Jesus is until His Word—the Living Word—takes hold of me. Then, it comes; the redirecting of the rule of my heart. The glance of my eye changes from me and myself, to Him!

Just try it. Try beginning your prayer time with thanksgiving.

When you feel stumped and frustrated, or just plain ol' nothing, start thinking of things you are thankful for. Thank God for who He is. You will discover that in this process, your eyes will soon be lifted up to Him and off of yourself. He is our greatest advocate and our source.

Isaiah 55:8 says: *"My thoughts are nothing like your thoughts, says the Lord, and My ways are far beyond anything you could imagine..."*

HAVE YOU MET
YOUR FISHERMAN?

He answered and said, "Whether He is a sinner or not I do not know.
One thing I know: that though I was blind, now I see.
John 9:25 NKJ

Walking along on a beach in Panama, my husband befriends a fisherman. They start sharing stories, and the fisherman talks of his fishing experiences in Mazatlán, Mexico. He loved his time there. Their conversation started to bring me down memory lane, as I had lived in Mazatlán also.

I thought to myself, *I have quite a different story than his. I don't have too many warm-fuzzies over that story.*

Don't we all have stories?

I've been sitting here thinking about how Jesus' act of love interrupted my lifestyle filled with drugs, alcohol, and dance clubs. I just had to see the world and experience it all. Then, I encountered a particular Fisherman.

Jesus, the "Fisher of Men."

John 9:25 says: *"The healed man replied, 'I have no idea what kind of man he is. All I know is that I was blind, and now I can see for the first time in my life!'"* To know this love, His love, this all-surpassing love was such a gift to me. It's an on-going gift. He never stops giving, loving, teaching, forgiving, showing us wisdom, giving us peace, or giving us counsel. It's so personal. He longs to have a relationship with you, anywhere, anytime. It doesn't have to be in a church. I personally met Him in my living room, with the sun streaming through the windows, and I still haven't forgotten.

His Love for you is perfect.

Let Jesus show you things you have never seen before, maybe longed to see, but couldn't put it into words. Something is just missing in your heart. We search for the elusive "thing" when all along, our Creator left that place vacant in your heart, just for Him alone.

Let Him sit there, in that seat of your heart. You will never regret it.

His Love for you is perfect.

It does not condemn or shame you, but His love opens the eyes of your heart to things you've never seen before.

"I was blind, but now I see."

MR. SMOOTH TALKER

*Being confident of this very thing, that He who has begun a good work
in you will complete it until the day of Jesus Christ.*
Phil 1:6 NKJ

The enemy of our soul? I call him Mr. Smooth Talker.

He says things like, "I'll take away the messy processes. I'll make it easier; you just have to conform to the ways of the world. Adapt to the culture around you, and fit in."

Messy processes are a part of our journey; everything about them makes our lives authentic and unique.

He will make something beautiful out of this process.

Don't give up on the process for the easy way out. Jesus loves for us to jump into His hands being like a piece of clay, letting Him mold us, wanting us to trust Him in the process. He will make something beautiful out of this process.

You will not feel condemnation, guilt, fear, or shame in His molding process. You might feel some pressure, some stretching, and definitely some hard places, as a piece of clay on the Potter's wheel. When He is done molding you, you will truly be a beautiful vessel.

What pours out of your newly formed vessel after this messy process? Truthfully, it won't be what you expected. It will be better. Welcome to newfound strength, courage, breakthrough, wisdom, perspectives, and thanksgiving.

Jesus always wants to make all things new. He wastes nothing. Mr. Smooth Talker, the enemy of your soul, wastes everything. The enemy loves to deplete you, deceive you, shame and condemn you.

God is creating a vessel of honor, to pour forth more of Him into you, and more of His attributes. Trust Him in the process. He is faithful.

Philippians 1:6 says: *"I pray with great faith for you, because I'm fully convinced that the One who began this glorious work in you will faithfully continue the process of maturing you and will put His finishing touches to it until the unveiling of the Lord Jesus Christ."*

2 Timothy 2:20-22 says: *"In a large house there are articles not only of gold and silver, but also of wood and clay; some are for special purposes and some for common use. Those who cleanse themselves from the latter will be instruments for special purposes, made holy, useful to the Master and prepared to do any good work. Flee the evil desires of youth and pursue righteousness, faith, love and peace, along with those who call on the Lord out of a pure heart."*

PANAMA CHRISTMAS

Have I not commanded you? Be strong and of good courage; do not be afraid, nor be dismayed, for the LORD your God is with you wherever you go.
Joshua 1:9 NKJ

In a little town in Panama, my husband and I spent the evening with brothers and sisters in Christ. We were on a mission trip and we had rented an apartment in a popular tourist area. It was Christmastime, and we sang Christmas carols, lit candles and remembered Christ the King, the Deliverer, the Messiah.

While we were away from our families, it was emotionally difficult, because we missed them with all our heart. Yet, on this night, we sang and worshipped with our family—our supernatural family. Every time we have traveled or been away from home, Jesus always meets us with His family.

If you are alone this Christmas season, I hope this page finds you. Jesus sees you; He loves you, and He has not forgotten you. He knows you, and He is with you. Always.

I have prayed over this page; that whoever reads it will receive comfort from these words; you are not alone. Joshua 1:9 says: *"For the Lord is with you wherever you go."* Isaiah 9:6 says: *"A child is born to us this day…and His name will be called Wonderful Counselor, Mighty God, Everlasting Father, Prince of Peace.."*

Remember this always; Jesus is here, *you are never alone.*

Run Your Own Race

Do you not know that those who run in a race all run but only one receives the prize?
Run in such a way that you may obtain it.
1 Corinthians 9:24 NKJ

I used to run track in high school, so I love this message in the Bible. In this verse, I can feel the coach talking to me, challenging me, training me.

I ran the 400 X 100-meter relay in which I carried a baton, and I passed it to the next runner in an area on the track called the exchange zone. But, one of my favorite races was the 4x400 meter relay.

You can't prepare or train for your teammate's part of their race; you must train for your part.

Both are a team event; therefore, you will have your own moment in this race; a defining moment that helps your team win their race. The important thing to remember is that you cannot prepare or train for your teammate's part of their race. You must train for your part. Everything in this race depends on two things; the hand-off in the exchange zone and speed. Focus hard, run fast, and don't miss the hand-off in the exchange zone!

I love this comparison to our exchange zones in life. We receive the baton—our faith—and we must give it away, as well, passing it on to the next runner. This is the challenge set before me: pass the baton to the next runner. It reminds me of the importance of training. Am I in the race, or on the sidelines? Am I showing up for practice or skipping training? I often think of my personal race, and this is the one I'm accountable for. I have passion and zeal for my race.

I want to pass my baton on to a generation behind me.

I've been in prayer for them. I believe in them. I am cheering them on. My heart skips a beat for this generation. I want to cheer them on from the sidelines. I want to coach them, encourage them, and believe for them when they can't believe for themselves.

To do this well, I must run *my* race. Not your race, not their race, but *my* race, and focus on my exchange. I want them to win their race!

One day I will be in the crowd watching the generation below me receiving their medals for the races they have won.

You must run your own race, the Race of Life. You have your own baton to carry. Don't miss the hand-off in the exchange zone! Run your race well!

Every day after you wake up, you're in training, and you become more equipped for your race. 1 Corinthians 9:24 says: *"Do you not know that in a race all the runners run, but only one gets the prize? Run in such a way as to get the prize."*

As the saying goes, "Live your life to the fullest, you must run your race as if you are sure to get the prize." Everyone who competes in the race goes into strict training. They do it to get a crown that will not last, but this race we call life doesn't offer a temporary prize; rather, we run it to get a crown that will last forever.

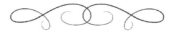

RACE TRAINING TIPS FROM JESUS:

- Meet with Me (Jesus) daily: we need to get to know each other. I know what you need to make a great participant in this race.
- Trust me; I'm a great coach—I'm your coach.
- Follow My lead: I have understanding and knowledge of your heart, mind, and soul. Therefore, I know how to teach you and show you precisely what you need to do. I will handcraft your race. Maybe it's endurance training today, or how to set your pace, when to keep your speed constant and when to accelerate.
- Downtime: You *need* downtime. Take it regularly with Me. I will teach you to rest, and rest in Me. Your muscles—physical and spiritual—need time to recover after a training session.
- Discipline: I know that word can be tough to hear at times. However, it really does work. It prepares you for *your* race. It produces steadfast results.

"*Now*," Jesus will say to you, "*go run your race with Me, passing your baton of faith to the next generation.*"

Got your baton? Ready, Set, GO!

TRUST HIM

Trust in the LORD with all your heart, and lean not on your own understanding; in all your ways acknowledge Him, and He will direct your paths.
Proverbs 3:5-6 NKJ

When you believe in God, you believe in *Him*, not you. When you walk with Him through hard seasons, He is still with you. He has not left the scene. Don't forget, He does things differently. His ways are far beyond our ways. He knows what He's doing. Sometimes it makes no sense to us.

His plans are far beyond our own goals or passions; His plans are expanded into eternity.

We've had to believe in things not yet seen, while praying and trusting in a supernatural God, a God that is not of this world. He does things differently than us. He looks at the whole picture, every portion. We see what's in front of us, maybe a few miles ahead. God does not see things in our time (a day, an hour, a year.) He sees everything in the expanse of eternity. Hang in there, continue to trust the One whose wisdom far exceeds our own. His courage—to the point of death—far exceeds our own personal courage. His plans are far beyond our own goals or passions; His plans are expanded into eternity.

I write this only for those who need to remember that Jesus never falls asleep His watch.

Ever.

Exercise your spiritual heart and meditate on scriptures each week. If you trust Him, it will get into the marrow of your bones, it will fill your heart with truth and faith, giving you renewed hope.

Speak them out loud. Put sticky notes on your bathroom mirror, reminding yourself of His ways, His sovereignty.

Romans 8:24-25: Hoping in what you cannot see: *"For this is the hope of our salvation. But hope means we must trust and wait for what is still unseen. For why would we need hope for something we already have? So, because our hope is set on what is yet to be seen, we patiently keep waiting for its fulfillment."*

Isaiah 55:8-9: My ways are not your ways: *"I don't think the way you think." "The way you work isn't the way I work." God's decree. "For as the sky soars above the earth, so the way I work surpasses the way you work, and the way I think is beyond the way you think."*

Proverbs 3:5-6: Trusting in Him to lead you: *"Trust in the Lord with all your heart, and lean not on your own understanding, in all your ways acknowledge Him, and He will direct your paths."*

Genesis 15:1 He is your reward! *".... Do not be afraid Abram. I am your shield, your exceedingly great reward."*

John 14:16: We have an advocate: *"And I will pray to the Father, and He will give you another Helper, that He may abide with you forever.... the Spirit of Truth"*

Psalm 28:7: He is our shield! *"The Lord is my strength and my shield; My heart trusted in Him, and I am helped; Therefore, my heart greatly rejoices, and with my song, I will praise Him."*

MARCY JOHNSTON

S ome would say that my testimony begins in quite a precarious fashion. Let me set the scene: a pregnant teenager is feeling immense "social pressure," and her parents are *very* displeased. A doctor, who is a "friend" to the young girl's father, has agreed to perform an abortion in his office. The doctor has turned on the suction device, but pauses and asks the mother of the girl to leave the room. He then asks the girl a life-giving question, "Do you really want to do this?"

"No!" she cries.

He reaches over and turns the suction off and says, "Okay. We won't."

So, here I am today.

I am a lover of life. One who is very thankful to be experiencing this beautiful world our Creator designed just for us. I am a believer and advocate for second chances, and I long to ask those life-giving questions that will bring others to the Face and Fullness of Life, Himself.

I believe in the table. It is a powerful place of connection and blessing. Feeding people is one of my love languages. As a wife, mother, sister, friend, and caterer, I get many chances to "love" people!

With much thanksgiving in my heart, my testimony shouts, *"Is anyone thirsty? Come and drink, even if you have no money! Come, take your choice of wine or milk—it's all free! Why spend your money on food that does not give you strength? Why pay for food that does you no good? Listen to Me, and you will eat what is good. You will enjoy the finest food. Come to Me with your ears wide open. Listen, and you will find life. I will make an Everlasting Covenant with you. I will give you all the unfailing love I promised to David."* Isaiah 55: 1-3

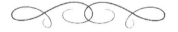

THE MANY FOOTHOLDS
OF THE ROCK

He is the Rock; His work is perfect; for all His ways are justice.
A God of truth and without injustice; Righteous and Upright is He.
Deuteronomy 32:4a NKJ

When we think of someone being a rock, words like strong, immovable, constant, and dependable come to mind. Many times, in the Bible, God is described as "The Rock." Probably the most familiar reference is Psalm 89:26: *"He is the Rock of my salvation."* Another way to say that would be, He is my Heavenly Father, God, who saves me!

My God is a Rock that has provided me with many sure footholds throughout my sixty-six years of living. In Exodus 17:6, God was a Rock of provision for the Israelites. He had instructed Moses to strike the rock, and water would flow from it so the thirsty people could drink and live. I have personally, miraculously, experienced God as the Rock of Provision.

As a family, we went through a financially difficult season. We had acquired a lot of debt from a failed business, and my husband was having a hard time finding solid work. Our house payment would be due soon, and just when we had exhausted all of our options, we received an anonymous money order in the mail. One time, we got a call from a local tire store and they told us that someone had paid for our tread-bare tires to be traded in for brand new ones!

But of all the testimonies of God's provision, the ones that blessed this mother's heart the most were the ones that provided for my kids. We did not have the finances for them to participate in the sports they loved, but they were continually provided for by anonymous benefactors. They always had the uniforms they needed, the soccer shoes or running shoes they needed, and all of the out-of-town travel expenses covered. It was a powerful testimony to our high school children; one they have not forgotten!

Psalm 40:2 talks about God being our Rock as a firm place to stand. He can lift us up out of "mud and mire" or bad situations and place our feet on Him, the Solid Rock.

When our youngest son was twelve months old, he contracted spinal meningitis. His symptoms had seemed like the flu, so we had not immediately taken him to the doctor's office. But after a full night of high fever and lethargy setting in, we took him to our family doctor. The concern that I saw on our physician's face was very alarming. He told us to go immediately to the ER, where we would meet up with a pediatrician and have further testing done. The next twenty-four hours were the longest I have ever experienced as we waited to see if the right antibiotic had been given to him. Because of the swift onset of his symptoms, there was no time to run tests that would pinpoint the type of treatment that was needed. Our pediatrician had to make a choice, and we had to pray and believe that it was the right choice. I prayed and prayed as we waited for our baby's response to the treatment. Fear would try to take me over, but a still, small voice would remind me of the promises God had already given me regarding our son's life.

I felt His comfort and presence as I lay by that baby boy through the night. God was my Rock, my solid place to stand, in the middle of scary circumstances. That baby boy is now twenty-eight years old and has had no residual effects from meningitis. We are still thanking and praising God, our Rock!

Where do you need to plant your feet this day? Our Rock has *many* beneficial footholds! Find the one you need today. He is ready to be there for you:

The Rock of Provision: Exodus 17:6

The Rock of Justice: Deuteronomy 32:4

The Rock of Refuge: 2 Samuel 22:2

The Rock of "A Firm Place to Stand": Psalm 40:2

The Rock that "Gets us above ourselves": Psalm 62:1

The Rock of Righteousness: Psalm 92:15

The Rock Who is always and will be: Isiah 26:4

The Rock that "smashes the idol": Daniel 2:34

The Rock to build on: Matthew 7:24-25

The Rock of Revelation: Matthew 16:18

The Rock of Conviction: Romans 9:33

WHAT IF

For God so loved the world, that He gave his one and only Son,
that whosoever believes in Him should not perish but have eternal life.
John 3:16 NIV

My husband and I were walking through our neighborhood when I noticed a scrappy-looking man pushing a Fred-Meyer shopping cart filled with an array of questionable treasures. We lived in a lower-income area, so it was not unusual to observe this scene.

I am sorry to say that I usually don't pay much attention; I am quick to give them a smile and just keep walking. But this man seemed to kick up some questions in my mind. I began to wonder how he had come to this place. What if his entire family has been killed in a car accident? What if he had been an executive of a company that folded?

"What if he was created in My image? And, what if I sent My son to die for him, too?"

What if he had a severe mental illness and couldn't get medication? What if addictions had alienated him from his friends and family? What if he was fearful of commitment? And then I heard a still, small voice in my heart say, *"What if he was created in My image? And, what if I sent My son to die for him, too?"*

Our world is full of people who seem lost, hopeless, poverty-stricken, mentally ill, or ravaged by addiction. We all have passed by them on the sidewalk or street corner. It is easy to become hardened to their presence, but is that what Father God would have us do? I don't think we always need to give them money or food, but a look into their eyes and a smile honors them as another human being, created in the image and likeness of God.

Years ago, I encountered a homeless gentleman who was asking for money. I sensed the Holy Spirit nudging me to stop and talk to him. I looked him in the eyes and told him I had no money but that I hoped his day got better. He smiled back at me and said, "My day is better already because you saw me."

Everyone has a story, and everyone needs to be seen. There is an old saying, "The ground is level at the foot of the cross." This is such a true statement and one to be pondered in moments when we cross paths with someone less fortunate. My prayer is that my eyes never become too casual to recognize the level ground. I must have needed a reminder that day. Thank you, Holy Spirit.

THANKSGIVING THAT ECHOES THROUGH THE AGES

Make a joyful noise to the Lord, all the Earth! Serve the Lord with gladness!
Come before His presence with singing! Know that the Lord, He is God! It is He who
made us, and we are His; we are His people and the sheep of His pasture.
Enter His gates with thanksgiving and His courts with praise!
Give thanks to Him; bless His name! For the Lord is good; His steadfast love
endures forever, and His faithfulness to all generations!
Psalm 100:1-5 NKJ

I remember hearing my grandmother expressing words of thanksgiving and acknowledging the Source of her provision. I recall her contentment as she prepared meals for her family, and how she would get so tickled by my grandfather's face after he had eaten corn-on-the-cob. In times of sorrow, she had the ability to speak of the "good things" in her life.

My desire is that my grandchildren will have memories of my expressions of gratefulness. May my words and actions continue to point to a faithful God, for generations to come!

The following family recipe is one of my favorite reminders of the "Goodness" of God.

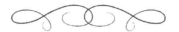

Gramma Fay's Oatmeal Cake

Ingredients

1 c. instant oats

1 1/2 c. boiling water

1 c. white sugar

1 c. brown sugar

1/4 c. oil

2 eggs

1 t. cinnamon

1 t. baking soda

1/2 t. salt

1 1/4 c. flour

Butter-caramel frosting

3/4 c. brown sugar

1/2 c. butter

2 T. milk

Mix in a saucepan and boil for one minute, then pour over the cooled cake.

In a large bowl, soften the oatmeal with the boiling water. When the oatmeal is cooled to lukewarm, add both sugars, oil, and the eggs...blend well. Mix the dry ingredients in a separate bowl and then add to the wet ingredients...mix well and pour into a greased 9 x 13 pan...bake at 350 degrees for 35 minutes. Cool slightly and top with butter-caramel frosting.

Enjoy!

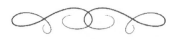

SHARLA JOHNSTON

L ooking back on my life, it's hard to imagine a time that I didn't have a relationship with God. I grew up in church. At home, Christian talk radio and Christian music was often the backdrop. Ever since I was little, God's gracious presence just felt real to me. Tangible, even.

As I got older, church summer camp was one of my favorite things of all. I was so deeply moved by the Holy Spirit in worship. I had such a desire for Him and compassion for others. That little camp chapel is where I first really experienced prayer, circled around with my friends. Our young hearts were so soft. We shared deeply, cried, and prayed for one another. God made my heart so big for them in prayer. I desired for everyone to be saved, healed, set free, everything so beautifully depicted in Isaiah 61:1-4.

A couple of years into a discipleship program, the Lord continued to show me the beauty of loving people through their brokenness. And while I could easily do it for others, I had difficulty accepting it for myself. I wanted to live right and do right and "be a good girl," but I was just a broken person falling short in my attitudes and emotions. I tried to keep it hidden and be pleasant and agreeable, but I felt as if I was clothed in filthy rags. It's difficult to grow and thrive when you're in hiding.

Later, as the team of Sanctioned Love began to grow, it became harder to hide as we worked so closely together in life and ministry. God, in His love and grace, began to teach me that there's great power in vulnerability with people who genuinely love and seek the best in you. It is a process, but I am thankful that I am not the same as I was when we all met those years ago. I'm beyond thankful that we are blessed with the opportunity to genuinely love others and watch our Heavenly Father give beauty from ashes.

FOR THE DISPLAY
OF HIS SPLENDOR

I have loved you with an everlasting love.
Therefore, with loving kindness, I have drawn you.
Jeremiah 31:3b NKJ

C an I have faith in pain? Hope in the outcome? What is it that remains with faith and hope? The greatest of all... Love.

Love wraps itself around all of it, and weaves a golden cord through the sometimes-fragile strands called faith and hope. Love bears all things.

You are a part of Him, but greater still, He is a part of you.

As the Potter sits at the wheel, His hands become fully immersed in the beautiful chaos. He closes his eyes, the humming of the wheel sounds like music to His ears. Spinning and spinning, water flies from His hands in an erratic dance. At times, the piece looks and feels so drastically misshapen, who could conceive what it will eventually become? One might question the design and function. But oh, the undeterred, unshaken Potter.

What a glorious mess!

Spackling clings to His brows and coats wisps of hair. He smiles, knowing they are there. You are part of Him, but greater still, He is part of you. He is putting something of Himself into you, into the design and unfolding of your life.

You shrink back, feeling thrown, or suffocated, but Love sees an outcome and pulls the slack into Himself. Without realizing, you breathe again, exhilarating, life-saving gulps.

Right there, amid the chaos, a beautiful masterpiece and grand display of His splendor emerges. He, Himself, has imparted qualities into you.

You are His beautiful workmanship.

SHAME HAS NO CURRENCY

They looked to Him and were radiant, and their faces were not ashamed.
Psalm 34:5 NKJ

My eyes were fixed upon her. There was something there. What was it? Nothing that could be seen with the natural eye, yet, it was undeniable. As if there was something heavy upon her back and shoulders.

I watched as she moved about, and she smiled as she spoke to people she encountered, but there was an unmistakable sadness beating rhythmically just below the surface. For those who cared to notice, it was clear this was a very familiar tightrope walk that she maneuvered cautiously to keep from losing her balance.

What was this weight, this pressure, keeping her locked in a precarious balancing act? Could it be rejection? Fear? Loss? Maybe. But this one's particular emotion had a name.

And this name was Shame.

You've probably seen her too. Maybe you are her. Most of us are, at one point in our lives or another.

Recently, I was ministering at a women's shelter and I felt the Lord speak a profound phrase to me: *"Shame has no currency."* You see, many people in the body of Christ carry shame. They have this idea of expectations and standards to live up to. When they fall short of those expectations, or when they sin, they take on a burden of shame in an attempt to make amends or atone for what they have done. Especially, if what they have done is known to others. As if to say, "I know I was wrong and I was bad. I know you won't forget it, so neither will I, and I'll try to do better, to *be* better, and to not mess up again. I will try to keep from letting others down."

Endless thoughts pound within our minds like a gavel beating; *shame on you, shame on you.*

But shame has no currency.

Shame is bankrupt.

Carrying it, tying it to your back, and climbing a ladder to the tightrope, allowing the gavel to beat its conviction over and over, can never satisfy the requirements of its sentence.

If it's a life sentence you are serving, then you have been wrongly convicted and today is the day for freedom! Today is the for redemption!

Psalm 34:5 says, *"Those who look to Him for help will be radiant with joy; no shadow of shame will darken their faces."*

Is shame a God-given emotion? No. It has no currency, so let it go and be free from the guilt.

FORGIVENESS PRAYER

FATHER, I RECEIVE THE FORGIVENESS YOU GIVE IN EXCHANGE FOR
MY SHAME WHEN I REPENT, BUT WHAT ELSE DO YOU WANT TO GIVE ME
IN EXCHANGE? EXCHANGE SHAME FOR FORGIVENESS,
GRATITUDE AND REDEMPTION?
WHO HAS MADE ME FEEL ASHAMED OR PUT SHAME ON ME?
HAVE I FORGIVEN THEM?
HAVE I CAUSED ANYONE ELSE TO FEEL SHAME?
IS THERE A WAY TO MAKE THAT RIGHT BETWEEN US?
IF THERE IS NO WAY TO MAKE IT RIGHT WITH THAT PERSON NOW,
MAKE IT RIGHT IN MY HEART BEFORE YOU, LORD.
FATHER, I RECOGNIZE THAT SHAME HAS NO CURRENCY AND
CARRYING IT DOESN'T HELP ME REPAY ANY WRONG THAT I HAVE DONE
OR MAKE UP FOR ANY LACK IN MYSELF THAT CAN ONLY BE FILLED BY
YOU.
YOU ARE THE ONLY ATONEMENT FOR SIN
AND I REPENT FOR _____.
I DECLARE TODAY THAT REPENTANCE DOES NOT CARRY SHAME ON
ITS BACK. IT IS A PURIFYING AND RESTORATIVE WORK.
I BOW MY HEART BEFORE YOU AND REPENT.
I NOW EXCHANGE MY SHAME FOR YOUR COMPLETE FORGIVENESS.
THANK YOU FOR HEALING MY HEART OF THE SHAME BROUGHT ON
ME BY OTHER PEOPLE. PLEASE FORGIVE ME FOR ANY SHAME I PLACED
ON ANYONE ELSE. PLEASE BRING THEM TO MIND AND GIVE ME THE
COURAGE AND HUMBLENESS OF HEART TO MAKE IT RIGHT WITH THEM.

JEN MEYERS

I was saved at the young age of eight, and I immediately began to share Jesus with everyone in my school. I fell in love with Him, and I wanted everyone to be saved.

Things weren't always as they seemed, and throughout the years, I became discouraged with trials and I walked away from the church, feeling frustrated and confused.

I ran from my problems for almost eleven years; from the time I was sixteen until I turned twenty-seven.

At sixteen, I starting drinking. At seventeen, I was raped, and by the age of twenty-four, I started using hard drugs. I had hit rock bottom and found myself facing the possibility of prison time. I was broken and I wore guilt and shame every day.

It was at this time in my life that God came in and rescued me. God took this person who was so bankrupt of love and devotion, completely broken, and He touched my life, turning me around with one encounter of His love and forgiveness.

Oh, His great faithfulness!

I found my way back into the doors of a church, where I cried through the whole worship service. I heard God say to me, "*I love you!*" and just as quickly, I fell back in love with my amazing Lord and Savior. He is just that patient and loving!

He took my mess and made it a message: "*It is by grace you've been saved, through faith...not by your works!*"

My heart was, and is for people to encounter the same love that saved my soul and experience a genuine, authentic relationship with Him and not get entangled in religious works.

I'd gotten caught up in a "works" mentality and lost the joy of my salvation, and now I found it in Jesus. He is the joy of my salvation.

Good works come out of an authentic relationship with Him. I have an amazing husband of twenty-one years, and we have three beautiful sons, and many other daughters and sons who we love with the same love of Jesus.

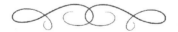

HIS WAYS

For as the heavens are higher than the earth, so are My ways higher than
your ways, and My thoughts than your thoughts.
Isaiah 55:9 NKJ

The enemy is shrewd and he uses trickery and lying. He comes to kill, steal, and destroy. He's not smart. I mean, think about it; he thought he won by sending Jesus to the cross, but what he really did was seal the deal for his own defeat, and Jesus' victory.

The enemy knows God's Word well, and this is why you must know Jesus more. You must know Jesus' heart, and all sides of it. Get to know His heart and the Word so well that you can differentiate between the enemy using the Word to manipulate you, and Jesus speaking to you.

Don't give up and don't give in to the enemy. Hold the line!

There are things you'll hope for, wish for, and pray for. There will be times your prayers start to be answered, and you'll probably be shocked at the way they are answered. Our God is creative, and He is a God with manifold wisdom[1]!

I have seen throughout my life how God does things and answers prayers in many creative ways, and on His timetable, working it all out for His glory and the greater good. He does things that will definitely surprise us. Some things take time, but if it were up to us, it'd be quick

---

[1] *The **wisdom** of **God** is "**manifold**" or "multifaceted." The manifold wisdom of God - Literally, "much-variegated." It means "greatly-diversified wisdom."*

and easy. In truth, it's going to cost our time and energy. Aren't you glad Jesus and His disciples considered the cost and pushed through times where it was hard and exhausting? They would go to the Father, just like Jesus did, and had their strength refreshed, renewed, and then continued to do precisely what it was they were called to do.

We must trust the Lord without depending on our own understanding, we must wait on Him and lean on His Word to find our strength.

The enemy knows God's Word well, and this is why you must know Jesus more.

Proverbs 3:5 says: *"Trust in the LORD with all your heart, and lean not on your own understanding."*

Isaiah 40:31 says: *"But they that wait upon the LORD shall renew their strength; they shall mount up with wings as eagles; they shall run, and not be weary, and they shall walk, and not faint."*

We rest in Him.

We trust Him when we know His character, His heart, and His will. Circumstances can't persuade us to give up, because we are already persuaded by Him. There are things we can rest assured in: that He is good, He is God, and He is not a man that He should lie. (Numbers 23:19a.) God does exactly what He says He'll do, and you can take that to the bank!

I'm grateful for the Word of God that is full of so many examples of victories, testimonies, and hard times where they had to fight, pray, and stand. Very rarely does it say it was simple, or they flew right through their troubles without having to trust God and wait on Him to renew their strength.

The battle belongs to the Lord. Jesus defeated the enemy on the cross. He said, *"In this world, you will have trouble, but take heart I have overcome the world."* John 16:3.

IS GOD THE SAME YESTERDAY, TODAY, AND FOREVER?

For I am the Lord, I change not.
Malachi 3:6 KJV

Has God changed? Or is He the very same God today that He was in Old and New Testament Times?

"For I am the Lord, I change not."

God is still healing, God is still delivering, God still has standards and He is still Love! God is still using people like He did in the Old and New Testament to do great and mighty works.

Jesus himself said, *"Greater things than these you will do and more."* (John 14:12.) Why? Because He said that He was going to the Father, and the Father was going to send the Holy Spirit, and whoever believes in Him would be given the power from the Holy Spirit to do these things to bring glory to the Father.

If you hear someone say, "This or that is not biblical," take a moment to discover it for yourself. Read, dig in! Talk to God and pray about it. There are many misconceptions that certain things ended in biblical times, when, in fact, we are still serving a living God. He hasn't gone anywhere. Our world is still covered by the same God and the same Holy Spirit. God has not changed; He has not stopped healing, He has not stopped using prophecy, He has not stopped using evangelists, and He has not stopped using people called Apostles[2], or those walking as Apostles.

There were biblical era Apostles, and today there are believing, walking, talking Apostles anointed by the same Holy Spirit to do the same things and more. Only a few things have changed, but not God.

All who believe have the Holy Spirit who lives within us to do great and mighty things, for the glory of God. The separation between God and sinful man was crushed by the sacrifice of Jesus' life on the cross. Those who believe and confess Jesus is the Son of God and receive Him as their Savior will have that power within. Let Him use you.

This world is where we live for a while, until He returns. Be wary of the misleading whispers from devious spirits that want you to shrink back from the call on your life.

We all have God-given, beautiful destinies. It's time to rise up and be used by God, and let His glory shine and be the light this world needs.

Our lives matter, our prayers matter.

Our prayers are powerful. Sometimes we don't see things happen right away or the way we want them to happen, but this is when we trust and wait.

Set your face like flint on Jesus. *"Resist the enemy, and he will flee."* (James 4:7.) What he has is nothing compared to what God has for you in His Kingdom and for your life.

---

[2] An Apostle is a vigorous and pioneering advocate or supporter of a particular policy, idea, or cause.

MELISSA NORRIS

To write my testimony in a short form turned out to be quite a challenge for me. Maybe because I see my life as a series of plucks and plunges, ebbs and tides, ups and downs, victories and losses. In my life's journey, I always seem to be in the need of His sovereign intervention. But the marvelous news is, this is Jesus' specialty!

Faithfully, He has so ever lovingly plucked me out of darkness and plunged me into the light of His love. His Holy Spirit calling me, and walking me right back to my God-given identity in Him, who is the Great I AM, and the Jesus living in me.

Isn't it true that God always seems to be about the business of us needing Him? His gentle and patient hands available and ready to help us, even in times of confusion, grief, or addiction. When we don't believe that anyone can see us, He whispers the words, *"I see you, I know you, and I love you."* He tells us we are His beloved, the redeemed of the Lord. Then, from this position of victory, He tells us to shout it out, *"Let the redeemed say so!"*

This is where my heart to minister and to write comes from. I have a burning desire to express to others that the Father sees them; that we are all lovingly visible to Him. For when we close our earthly eyes and open our spiritual eyes to each other through the vision of the Holy Spirit, we will see each other covered in Christ's blood.

We will see the cross. This vantage point pours passion into my hunger. A hunger to rejoice in the power of prayer, to share words of knowledge, to encourage by fellowship. For when two or more come together seeking Him, we have unity. When we have unity, we have liberty. Where there is liberty, the Spirit has room to move. We become a united chorus of Jesus-lovers, singing praises of victory to our Jesus.

Now this place, where the redeemed are saying so, is everything to me. My Faithful Father will be my epitaph.

LIVING WATER

*Jesus answered and said to her, "If you knew the gift of God,
and who it is who says to you, 'Give Me a drink,' you would have asked Him,
and He would have given you Living Water.*
John 4:10 NKJ

While driving on a local highway one morning, I was praying and praising the Lord, and the Holy Spirit whispered to me, "Empower people with knowledge today." Immediately, I knew that the Holy Spirit was referring to the Living Word. This statement was about speaking the love of Christ, and sharing the Good News.

With suddenness, this statement came with a specific picture, instantly downloaded to my heart in unison to the words. The picture was an image of pouring Holy Water of the Holy Spirit over the minds, bodies, and into the mouths of others. In this image, many of the receivers didn't even know that it was Jesus or the Living Words of His scripture. However, because the offering was a refreshing drink, wet with encouragement and love in the midst of their dry and thirsty life, they drank. And remember, even believers can get dehydrated while walking their road of life.

For it is only by His Divine Love purchased on the cross that we can empower anybody.

To those who were receiving, this water simply appeared to be just water, for they did not all know the source of this Divine provision. They just drank out of thirst. But for me, I was to facilitate in the giving of a free drink. The free drink of encouragement. The knowledge that Jesus Himself by the power of the Holy Spirit, is always wanting to pour His love life into our vessels. I was to simply share the wealth of God's free gift given to me, to share from my own cup, to share with my own eyes that God sees them, even if it's just in the gift of a glance.

To share by my presence from time spent in Jesus' presence, and from that place one can receive the free gift of peace.

To share my reflection, because Jesus Himself makes us a light on a hill.

To share my garment of love which was purchased for me on the cross by His blood. This is a garment that anyone could receive.

I was told in the car that day to empower others, to be like my Lord, a free drink-offering of truth.

This was the drink, the supernatural fluid, the liquid I was to share, the power of His knowledge, the giving away of His Love and Hope. For it is only by His Divine Love purchased on the cross that we can empower anybody.

He is all power.

He is all love.

He is the Gift.

John 3:16 says: *"For God so Loved the world that He gave His one and only Son, that whoever believes in Him shall not perish but have eternal life."*

SNAPSHOT

The law of his God is in His heart; none of His steps shall slide.
Psalm 37:31 NKJ

I love it when you're reading the Word of God, and the Holy Spirit creates a pause. A stop-right-there, go-back-and-take-a-snapshot moment. A press-the-image-button-in-your-mind moment. A "save it" moment for teaching.

It could be a single word on the page, or a whole paragraph that's shouting your name. But somehow, you know that deep down, it's a Holy Spirit teaching time.

How do you know it's a teaching time?

Well, my challenge to that question is this: how do you know it's *not* a teaching time?

Isn't it true that we sometimes allow a moment of pause to fill up with words such as, "um," or "maybe?" Or a "how can I know for sure that this isn't just a *me* thought?"

Why do we err on the doubting moment rather than the assuming moment of the Holy Spirit? Isn't He able to speak to us? To those who are willing to have ears to hear what the Holy Spirit is saying?

Is He not our Teacher? Our Comforter? Our Guide?

Haven't we been told by Jesus Himself that we would not be orphaned but filled with His Holy Spirit as a promise that we belong to Him?

I would rather believe to my best ability that He is speaking to me than to doubt that He is unable to guide me to His truths. We must believe that Holy Spirit is living inside of us for this amazing purpose. He is called to be our helpmate by our Father. By the position of the Trinity, He is our Teacher.

The great blessing, the best-of-all-thoughts is that He loves to teach us, He loves to guide us, and He loves to comfort us.

I urge you to believe that it is He who is saying, *click it, save it, and digest it.*

The message of Psalm 37:1-40 are the words to the righteous, and the heritage to those who believe in the Lord. When I read this amazing Psalm of David's, I heard the echo of so many powerful words. Words like: Trust, Commit, Rest, Wait, Delight, Meek, Peace, and Dwell. All words to live by, all words to study.

By the position of the Trinity, He is our Teacher.

But in that moment of reading, I was sent to my knees for a pause. I was to stop right there, in order to digest these words into the depth of my soul.

Words I was to save.

A snap shot to be used by Holy Spirit.

What about you? Can you too be encouraged by these simple words?

Stop, take a snapshot, press the image button in your mind, and save it for the Holy Teacher's teaching.

PONDERING PARADOXES

And Jesus answered them, saying, "...He who loves his life will lose it, and he who hates his life in this world will keep it to eternal life."
John 12:23-25 NKJ

W e have all, at some point, pondered the paradoxes of serving our Lord, for the whole of Christianity is a paradox life.

As we view our spiritual walks here on Earth, we can see what appears to be contradictory. As Christ-followers, we live by Jesus' teachings, and these teachings are so often contrary to commonly shared opinions and understandings of men. This list is just an example of the narrow way:

- When we see in the Spirit, we see unseen things.
- Do you want to be free? Then become a bond slave of God.
- In conquering, we must first be yielding.
- We reign when we are serving.
- To be strong is to be found in weakness.
- Our triumph can be found in our defeat.
- We are made great by becoming small.
- To die is to gain.
- We are exalted when we are humbled.
- We become wise by being fools for Christ's sake.

This is just an example of the narrow way. It is direct and straightforward to lay out the biblical truth of the paradoxes that we live by as believers. We know as we read it that our journey between the flesh and the Spirit are clearly evident. Take courage, Friend, for we are not bi-polar as it may seem, but rather gloriously, we are working out our salvation in Christ.

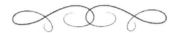

HUMBLED BUT HUNGRY

Lord, I come to you and drop to my knees.
To climb down the mountain of my own mind, and to advance up
the mount of your Holy Throne.
Humbled but hungry.
Bringing my bundle of praise, and
emptying my bag of supplications.
To ask you, Holy Spirit, to open my eyes so my focus
is closed to the world, and fixed on Your gaze.
This is where I drop to my knees.
Humbled but hungry.
To wait upon your sovereignty, Lord, with an activated faith.
Submitted to nothing less than Your Will.
Standing in hope, not deferred.
Humbled and hungry.
Your highway makes my crooked road straight.
You're the narrow way, Jesus, to the

massive dimensions of eternity.
May I give You my life of emptiness so
that I may receive Your abundance?
Your mercies are true.
May my inadequacies be exchanged
by Your filling, Holy Spirit.
Your power converging with my weakness.
I come humbled and hungry.
My flesh, freshly fasted for the
satisfaction of eating the bread of life.

When I wrote this messy poem and not-so-private prayer, I did not knowingly or intentionally do so with the teaching of biblical paradoxes in mind. Instead, in the birthing of it, I poured out my heart by the faithful revelation of the Holy Spirit. I was, indeed, seeking to walk the higher, narrower road of peace in the paradoxes of truth.

Hebrews 4:12 says: *"For the Word of God is living and powerful, and sharper than any two-edged sword, piercing even to the division of soul and spirit, and of joints and marrow, and is a discerner of the thoughts and intentions of the heart."* Take an opportunity to truly ponder the power of the paradoxes we face, and the practice of their truths. Use them as instruments of encouragement, and may you find bravery in their challenges.

Some well-known paradoxes in scripture that I've meditated on are:

- James 4:10 teaches being *exalted through humility.*
- 2 Corinthians 12:10 speaks of *strength through weakness.*
- Acts 20:35 shows us that we *receiving through giving.*
- Romans 6:18 Our *freedom comes through servitude.*
- Philippians 3:7-8 To comprehend that we are *gaining in the losing.*
- John 12:24 The greatest real mystery is that we are *living through dying.*
- Matthew 10:39 To remember that we *find through losing.*

SAY YES TO YOUR STORY

I will praise You for I am fearfully and wonderfully made; Marvelous are Your works, and that my soul knows very well.
Psalm 139:14 NKJ

I am a story that's been written before time.

I am a story made into a rhyme.

If you were to read me in the pages of a book, what would it say?

Am I a Little Miss Much-Afraid?

Or have I turned in my man feet for Hinds' feet,

whose hooves can bound to high places with Christ?

Have I developed a story worth writing in a book?

One that has dots over i's and t's that are crossed?

Or with sentences that don't have periods at the end?

Where the phrase "growing weary in the waiting"

is just a pause for more?

Maybe my story has paragraphs that say something like this:

My daughter has a hungry heart for endurance, and the obedience to go up high. She knows that her Comforter is a Stag who rides in those high places of peace. Her feet are being transformed into hooves, strong as bronze, and gleaming with the bright fruit of Joy. She is now able to bound from rock to rock as the trail crisscrosses up the slope. And with newfound ease, she can work her way back down again; down to the pastures of provision and rest.

I am a story that's been written before time.

I am a story made into a rhyme.

My story will be read aloud one day, and may my Savior shout out
to say with His words of praise, that His Holy Spirit was able to make
a Doe out of Little Miss Much-Afraid.

A Gazelle that grazes with her eyes on a hill,
just waiting to prance once again with her Buck.

"For your Maker is your Husband;
the LORD of Hosts is His name." Isaiah 54:5

I wrote this poem at an important moment of pondering the story of my life. I had read the famous book, *Hinds Feet on High Places,* by Hannah Hurnard, and it was so instrumental that it changed my life.

God's timing is amazingly right. I had been delivered by His faithful hand out of my alcoholism. Now, I am walking with my mouth wide open, shouting out the glory of "Let the Redeemed say so!"

I could hardly contain my praise for Him, for He willingly and patiently rescued me from myself and set me back onto His Rock. The power of our life's testimonies will, indeed, be laid out by Christ Himself, for all to see.

Many years ago, I taught a simple Bible study on Mary, Jesus' mother. It was titled "Obedience" for she is an amazing example of a biblical role model. She was a young Jewish girl, a lover of God, mother to our Lord, and a faithful and obedient disciple. Part of Mary's story can be read today on the pages of the Bible, but, oh, I can only imagine "the more" of her story that we will see one Glorious day.

The intimate journeys of her heart and how she must have walked with the heartbeats of joy and pain. A woman who said "yes" to her journey and the pages of her life. Willingly, she surrendered to the words spoken to her, words that had been written before the time of man began.

It is my heart's desire to encourage all of us as individuals to fall in love with our journey; our unique story of how Jesus has called us to the pages that God Himself has written over our lives. May we choose to be books of faithfulness, redemption, obedience, and honor to our King.

I encourage you to take time and explore the following verses, to help you say "yes" to your story:

- Read Luke Chapter 1:1 through Chapter 2:40
- Blessed and Favored. Luke 1:26-33. We, too, have been chosen to tell a story of blessing and favor with our lives, no matter how small we may feel.
- Luke 1:31-34. Mary does ponder the possibility. But she, unlike Zacharias, does not doubt the power of God's ability to perform the miraculous. May we, too, remember that faith does not always make sense, and to not be afraid to trust the Divine Will of God.
- Luke 1:35. The beauty and comfort given to Mary by the angel, that the Holy Spirit would come in power. He would do the work. We can also trust that the Holy Spirit is with us, helping us to perform the tasks at hand.

- Luke 1:36-37. The angel also gives Mary some holy encouragement in telling her about Elisabeth's miracle. For with God, nothing will be impossible. This Clarian call was not just for Mary but for us all.
- Luke 1:38 (My favorite.) *"Behold the maidservant of the Lord! Let it be to me according to Your Word."* May we all yearn to have a heart like young Mary's heart. Full of willingness and bravery.
- Let us conclude this time with Mary, who is a role model of a heart that was responsive to her God. I believe she must have practiced this scripture wholeheartedly. *"In all your ways acknowledge Him, and He will direct your paths."* Proverbs 3:16.

USING THE WORD "BUT"

But, those who wait on the LORD shall renew their strength; they shall mount up on wings like eagles, they shall run and not grow weary, they shall walk and not grow faint.
Isaiah 40:31 NKJ

Many of us have read this passage multiple times. They're such powerful words of encouragement for every believer, and favorite go-to scripture in times of trouble. This past summer, I was in a difficult place of pressure. I had many things on my plate and was about to make a huge life change. So, when this passage came through my headphones while hiking one day, I knew I needed to get home and take it to prayer.

I sat down in my prayer room and opened my Bible to read Isaiah 40. As I was reading, the Holy Spirit started His download of intimacy between Faithful Father and me. It went something like this:

"Melissa, haven't you known, and haven't you heard Me tell you that I am with you always? I am the Alpha and Omega of your life. I know all about you, I understand it all. Your weaknesses and fears may seem true, but I am your strength. Run to me, run to my Word, for I am strong no matter your weakness."

And, as only Papa God can, by the power of divine love He gave me an admonition to put my big-girl-panties on. My response was, of course, "Yes, Papa."

However; He was not done, and the learning was about to begin. Papa God's next statement was something like this:

"Ok then. I want you to ponder this word. The word is...BUT."

It was like a light bulb lit up and brought me into a huge study session. Hours later, I had piles of wealth around this word, this three-letter word, "BUT."

It was as if the word became a hinge on a door.

A joint to swing wide a conversation.

One designed to stop the listener in his tracks.

For it is weighty enough to shift the whole perspective of thought, as in Isaiah 40:31: *"BUT, those who wait on the Lord shall renew their strength."*

This three-letter word can become our pinnacle word for our declarations in Christ. It takes us on a fast track to the victories won on the cross. Unfortunately, the world uses this word a lot, too. "But this," and "but that." It's a classic tool of our enemy as well. Think about Adam and Eve in the garden, Samson, or even King Saul. We read in Hebrews 11 about our patriarchs who used the word BUT to stand in their faith, putting truth above their fears and circumstances.

> **BUT those who wait on the Lord shall renew their strength.**

And didn't Satan try to use that trick with the word "BUT" against Jesus while in the wilderness? See Matthew 4:1-11. In verse 4, it says, "But He (Jesus) answered him (Satan) and said, '*It is written...*'" Then, as if Satan didn't get the point, he came back at Jesus with the challenge again; only this time, he used the scripture to mock Jesus. And still, Jesus uses the words "*It is written.*"

The enemy is pushy!

On the third time around, Jesus stands in His authority and states, "*Away with you, Satan! For it is written...*"

I believe that Satan is always using the word BUT against our God and His Word, because he is always after us and our hope in Christ. Trying to argue with us so we don't wait in faith on our Lord. This is where we need to put the brakes on.

We need to turn the table on our enemy and say the word BUT right back. To use the scripture and stand in who we are in Christ. We have been given a whole arsenal of identity. Don't argue with Satan about it. Jesus didn't! Just stand in the wait, with your faith and expectancy. Use the word BUT as a platform to stand on. Remember that the word BUT is a hinge, a tool designed for you, so that you can push open the door and walk through to the power of God's Word. Take another look at Isaiah 40:27-31.

As if I was not already so full, the Lord went on and said, "*Melissa, I have another word for you; the word is SHALL, and this is your promise word.*"

Just think about it; the Bible uses the word SHALL about 8,000 times. Many times, it's used to lead you to a promise, a fact, a position, or an identity that we have in Christ. In Isaiah 40:31, the word SHALL is used four times. "*But those who wait on the Lord SHALL renew their strength, they SHALL mount up with wings like eagles, they SHALL run and not be weary, they SHALL walk and not faint.*"

Now, when fear knocks on my door and the enemy tries his BUT approach, I take the power words of BUT and SHALL and put them to work for a great exchange. I am to simply swing wide the Door of Truth (Jesus is the Door and the Truth) and walk in with the strength to my Papa God.

Fear is always going after the Word in us.

Fear tries to get us to question a God-given promise.

Fear wants to speak half-truths to us to bring confusion.

Fear wants us to take everything personally, as an attempt to divide us and conquer our emotions.

Fear is always, always, after our identity in Christ.

Fear wants us to confirm fear, with fear.

When fear rears its ugly head and Satan wants to confuse you or take you down by questioning God and His Word, stand up, swing the "Door of Truth" wide open and walk boldly into Papa God's presence, and tell Satan, *"It is written!"*

NANETTE OLESON

A s I sat at my desk preparing to write my testimony, The Holy Spirit brought to remembrance an incident marking the beginning of my connection to the Father of Love: I saw myself as a four-year-old crying on my tear-stained bedspread, telling my stuffed animal that someday, we would run away together. I don't remember the reason for my punishment and banishment to my room (which were frequent occurrences), but God reminded me of this forgotten time and the prayers I cried as a child, and told me, *"That was the day you became endeared to Me."* Later, at nine-years old at a Baptist camp, I accepted Jesus as my Lord and Savior. At another camp when I was twelve, the Holy Spirit entered in a tangible manifestation, and we were all filled in the midnight hour gathering with loud songs of rejoicing. Thus, began my friendship with God and the Holy Spirit.

This relationship carried me through the dark tumultuous times of adolescence as the caregiver for an alcoholic stepmother who would later abandon me. I was left caring for my bipolar father and drug-addicted brother. I saw no way out. I could not desert them to join a Christian community and attend college. Yet, just like the Hebrew people under Pharaoh, God engineered a supernatural deliverance. I later pursued my dream of becoming a Special Education teacher and school counselor.

In fifty years of sharing life with Christ, I have amassed a vast list of dreams fulfilled. Perhaps the most visible began materializing fifteen years ago. At the time, I was a school counselor and organized many extracurricular opportunities for children, especially in art. My passion was that each child would discover their unique giftedness. Little did I know, mine was buried deep beneath the surface. I loved beautiful art, but I, like many would say, "I can't even draw stick people!" Then, a chance encounter with a 75-year-old woman changed everything. This stranger offered to come to my house and teach me to paint. An artistic whirlwind began, propelled by a passion for becoming an accomplished artist.

During this journey with God, I confidently attest to His faithfulness as we wait for the fulfillment of dreams. Family members are saved, relationships restored, gifts uncovered as we position ourselves in hope-filled waiting.

WAITING

Wait on the Lord, be of good courage, and He will strengthen your heart.
Wait, I say on the Lord.
Psalm 27:14 NKJ

T he title of this painting is *Waiting*.
Perhaps the heron is waiting for a mate, waiting for a change in the weather, or waiting for its next meal. Its eyes are fixed, and its body held motionless in hushed calmness.

Much of our lives are spent waiting. It might be for a loved one's recovery, health, salvation, revival, or simply waiting in the grocery checkout line. Our peace comes from settling into the moment and posturing ourselves with hopeful expectancy.

When Jesus approached a sick man waiting at the pool of Bethesda, the man felt hopeless. Even though a part of him knew that an angel would come and stir the waters and someone would be healed, he could not imagine that the healing would be for him, as he had no friends to put him in the pool, and others stepped in before him. He was alone, abandoned, and lost to self-deprecation, but in that place, Jesus met him in an unexpected way. Like the man at the pool, if we stand still and wait with the small faith we have, Jesus will meet us in unforeseen ways.

One of my biggest sacrifices as a young adult was to give up the dream of enrolling in an out-of-state university that was near a Christian community I had wanted to join. I made the difficult decision to stay and support my father rather than pursue this dream. It was fifteen years later, while attending a Christian university in Virginia with a scholarship and an even more amazing, paid *year's* leave of absence from my public teaching, that God reminded me of my previous sacrifice and now the fulfillment of my dream.

In many of the most difficult places in my life, God has met my "waiting" in unexpected ways.

My father was a brilliant person with a troubled mind, somewhat eccentric but laced with generosity. My mother was not in the picture, so the responsibility of his care and our home rested on me. As a young child, all the way into adulthood, my deepest prayer and cry was that my father would enter into God's peace.

The ultimate answer to my prayer came at his death bed. After his heart attack and three days on life support with a decision needing to be made about continuation, I cried out to the Lord, "God, I have waited all these years to know my father entered into peace. Will You confirm this with a sign that he will sit up in bed? But, even if You don't give me the sign, I am going to believe because You are faithful, and I have staked my prayers and tears believing this." Just as my father's EKG flattened for a final time, while I was holding his hand, he sat up in bed, looked to Heaven, and put his head down.

The Bible encourages us: *"Let us not grow weary in doing good, for at the proper time we will reap a harvest if we do not give up."* Galatians 6:9. I received the honor of not only seeing my father enter God's kingdom, but also leading my 83-year-old mother to the Lord, and introducing my 85-year-old father-in-law to Jesus.

Waiting is not passive, but an action filled with expectation and hope. Proverbs 8:34 says, *"Blessed is the man that hears Me, watching daily at My gates, waiting at the posts of My doors."*

As you wait on the Lord, position yourself in faith and peace, knowing that He will hear and answer your prayers.

RHEYMA
OOSTERMAN

I grew up in church; if the doors were open, my family was there. As the years went on, I attended X-ray school, and then began working as an X-ray technician. I continued to go to church, but for some reason, it left me feeling empty. Church seemed to teach me that "God was the answer," but that answer just wasn't working for me.

All my life, I longed to be loved and accepted just as I was, but that yearning seemed to elude me no matter how hard I tried to find satisfaction. It wasn't that people didn't love or accept me; I was unable to receive it because I never felt worthy of being loved. I always felt that I had to earn it, and I worked my fanny off trying.

Over the years, I developed multiple mental lists; how to be a good daughter, how to be a good sister, how to be a good friend, and of course, how to be a good Christian (which is difficult when all you have is religion and not relationship!) My belief was that I would be lovable and acceptable by doing all of those things on my lists.

When I got married and had kids, I added more lists; how to be a good wife, and how to be a good mother.

Society, media, the "Barbie-era" and church *helped* me know what to put on my lists. As my lists became longer, they became heavier and harder to maintain until one day, I just couldn't carry the burden anymore, so...

I quit.

I literally curled up into the fetal position by my woodstove, and I quit life. The result was a total and complete emotional, mental, and physical breakdown. I could no longer maintain my lists.

Fast forward through several, very tough years. My daughter suggested that I listen to Dan Molher, a renowned pastor who preaches the gospel of salvation, healing, blessing and deliverance, and,

OH.

MY.

WORD.

He spoke of Christianity in a way that I had never heard before. I knew in my heart this was the authentic, real-deal Christianity that I had been searching for all my life.

Enter Sanctioned Love.

Were they the answer? No. People are never the *answer*, but they definitely had the authentic real-deal-relationship-with-Jesus I had been searching for. God, of course, had been working behind the scenes the whole time.

During the time that I was looking for a way to cope with my struggles, God chose the *perfect* therapist for me. She saw me. She heard me. Not just my words, but she heard my *heart*. Then, as an assignment from my therapist, I volunteered at the Cancer Center.

Lo and behold, guess who was working there?

Marcy Johnston and Lynda Renne of Sanctioned Love.

As our friendship grew, they both became a safe place to ask questions and I finally began to find the answers I had been searching for.

I now have that authentic real-deal-relationship-with-Jesus, personally. I'm still asking questions, not *how* to get it, but how to *authentically walk it out*.

And now, I'm asking Jesus.

SEEK YE FIRST

Seek ye first the kingdom of God.
Matthew 6:33a NKJ

In my favorite devotional book, *Jesus Calling: Enjoying Peace in His Presence*, this morning, Jesus, you said, "*Seek Me, above all else. Anything else is an idol.*"

I pondered this a while, and like a puzzle piece clicking into place, I began to realize the meaning behind His words.

I closed my eyes, lifted my chin to the heavens, and asked Papa God, "Is that where fasting comes in? Fasting is a sacrifice. Sacrifice is giving up something I enjoy in order to grow closer to You. Right? Is that it?"

He responded with His wisdom.

He was teaching me that the sacrificial "thing" becomes less, and He—Papa God—becomes more. That "thing" is not erased from my life, but its importance is lessened more and more until it's a blessing. A gift, not a necessity.

You, Papa God.

You, Jesus.

You, Holy Spirit, are the *only* necessity.

That's why Jesus said to me, "*Seek Me first, Rheyma, and everything else will be added unto you.*"

BE STILL
BEFORE THE LORD

Be still before the LORD and wait patiently.
Psalm 37:7 NKJ

Lord, you said, *"Give yourself fully to this new adventure with Me."*

But, how do I do that practically, Papa?

You said,

Sit.

Wait.

Listen.

Let go.

Don't try to control things.

Don't try and fix it.

Take your hands off the situation.

Instead, spend time being still with Me, listening.

Move on the Holy Spirit's prompting.

Not on what *you* think is right.

"For My thoughts are not your thoughts, nor your ways My ways," declares the Lord. *"For as the heavens are higher than the earth, so are My ways higher than your ways, and My thoughts than your thoughts."* Isaiah 55:8-9.

OFF TO CLASS I GO

"I will instruct you and teach you in the way you should go," says the LORD.
Psalm 32:8a NKJ

In Your Word, Papa God, You say You'll teach me, guide me, and counsel me, but You don't say you'll make my decisions for me (although I wish You would.) It's difficult at times, but I've come to realize that my decisions are my choice, and it's up to me to make the choice and put what I've learned into action.

To follow or not to follow? That is the question.

Actually, that is the decision...*my* decision.

So, if I want You to teach, guide, and counsel me—and I do—I need to go and spend time with You "in class."

Sometimes I need to just sit and listen.

Sometimes I need to take notes.

Sometimes I need to ask questions.

Sometimes I need to take what I've learned and act on it.

And then, sometimes I need to come back to class and refine it, or redefine it, or simply refresh my memory. And boy, do I need that! If I don't spend one-on-one time with You, getting to know Your ways, getting to know Your voice, getting to *know You*, I am just following me.

Thank you, Papa God, for making sure that Your door is always open and Your office hours are 24/7/365.

PAPA, YOU ARE MY HEART

In God is my salvation and my glory;
the Rock of my strength, and my Refuge, is my God.
Psalm 62:7 NKJ

Not, *where* is my heart focused.

But where *is* my heart?

Who has my heart?

Papa God, has my heart.

It is safe with Him.

It is not safe on my sleeve.

It is not safe with someone else.

I can't trust anyone else with all my hopes and dreams.

It is only safe, secure, and whole with You, Papa God.

I can fight, give, and love from a spot of safety, a spot of strength, a spot of secure-ness.

Papa, You are never depleted!

Your Love endures forever!

Thank you, Papa.

PUZZLE PIECES

"For My thoughts are not your thoughts, nor are your ways My ways," says the LORD.
Isaiah 55:8 NKJ

We look, and we look, and we look.

We think it through, and attempt to reason it out. Some pieces look like they will fit; they have all the right curves and colors, but no matter how hard you try turning it, pushing it, pounding it, it just won't fit!

Sometimes you need to walk away for a bit instead of trying and failing, failing, failing. Failure leads to frustration, which gives way to anger, which ultimately leads to our less-pretty side.

Walking away doesn't mean putting one foot in front of the other. No, walking away means to take your hands off the situation. Stop trying to control it or force it, but allow God to work on the puzzle without your help.

Stop trying to control it or force it, but allow God to work on the puzzle without your help.

Later you come back, and one of several things happens: All of a sudden, you see the missing piece you've been looking for...Hallelujah! Thank you, Jesus! Or, "Someone" (Papa God), has put another piece in place, giving you more information to now look for the piece. Or possibly, "Someone" (Papa God), has found the missing piece that fits and put it into place, allowing you to continue on with the puzzle.

Take a moment to ponder that the missing piece that fits has actually been on the table all along. There were so many other pieces among this one, many appearing to be similar, you could not see it. Many times, we tend to overlook the missing piece that fits because it doesn't look like "the piece" that fits.

PAPA, IT'S YOUR YOU-NIVERSE, NOT MINE

We are like common clay jars that carry this glorious treasure within, so that the ordinary overflow of power will be seen as God's not us.
2 Corinthians 4:7 tPt

Papa, forgive me for being *so* selfish, living in my own little you-niverse. It's not all about me. It's all about You.

A word from Holy Spirit to me: "Rheyma, your world gets smaller and smaller the more you focus on you, and what *you think* your heart needs, and how those needs aren't being met. How you wrongfully think everyone—*really Rheyma? Everyone?* —is forgetting about you, which in turn zaps your energy, mentally, emotionally, and physically."

Papa, turn my water, which is getting all yucky, into wine.
Your wine.
The best wine you have.
And let me be the ordinary clay pot You use to serve it to anyone
You choose.
I'm your vessel, and it's Your wine.
Forgive me, Papa, for allowing clutter, dirt, sticks, and stones, clog
up, defile and poison my water.
Take Your net—although You will probably need a backhoe—and
scoop out all the debris so I can have clear, clean water that You can
turn it into beautiful, refreshing, life-giving wine.
The choice is before me every day.
Choose You and Your YOU-niverse,
or, choose me and my little earth-bound you-niverse.

WHERE THE RUBBER MEETS THE ROAD

Blessed is the man who trusts in the Lord, and whose hope is in the Lord. For he shall be like a tree planted by the waters, which spreads out its roots by the river...
Jeremiah 17:7-8a NKJ

Where does the rubber meet the road in my walk with you, Jesus? That's what I would like to know. Otherwise, my walk is worthless. I want to put my walk with Jesus into practice. I want it to mean something. Otherwise, I'm just putting on a show, like a show dog. And what good is that? Hours and hours of work, learning to walk right, sit right, *look* right. All costing tons of money to accomplish what? To be the perfect "show dog" and win a prize that doesn't do anything except hang on my wall so everyone can know just how "perfect" and wonderful I am?

Been there, done that, left me empty.

No, I'd rather be that hairless rabbit, the one from the children's story, *The Velveteen Rabbit.*

We walk by faith, not by feelings.

Walking with Jesus isn't a performance. In fact, ninety percent of our walk with Jesus is unseen. What makes a tree strong, and able to withstand the storms? It's the hidden root system. And yes, we have all heard that in a sermon at church. But what I didn't hear was how that root system takes time,

128

energy, and proper nutrients to grow strong. It just doesn't happen without those things.

So why do we think a deep walk with Jesus can "just happen?" Just by going to church, listening to sermons, singing praise songs, and raising our hands? Oh, and going up to the altar for healing? Yes, all good stuff, but is there a private heart-surrendering time with Jesus? Trusting. Releasing. Letting go of our life for Jesus' life? That is not done in the market place. No, that is done in the quiet, secret place of the heart. Just me, Jesus, Holy Spirit, and Papa God. And it takes multiple, on-going sessions, not a once-and-done thing.

We walk by faith, not by *feelings.*

Take every thought captive. Refuse to give Satan's lies, half-truths or schemes any power. Kick them back into his face!

Psalm 1:2-3a RPV (Rheyma's personalized version): *"But my delight is in the law of the Lord, and in God's law, I want to meditate day and night. Then, and only then, will I be like a tree that is planted by rivers of water, that brings forth fruit in its season."*

WORDS

Death and life are in the power of the tongue, and those who love it will eat of its fruit.
Proverbs 18:21 NKJ

Holy Spirit, not only do I want to hear You more and be more sensitive to Your voice, I want to be more *aware* of Your voice.

To think of You first.

So I am asking You, "What do You want me to do in this situation? What do You want me to say, or not to say, before I start flapping my lips and tongue?"

Words have power. Incredible power; way more power than we know or even realize.

My words have power, and Your words, God, *definitely* have power! You created things with Your words. My words can't necessarily make an object, but, they can make a difference.

They can open up a situation.

They can calm fears.

They can open hearts.

They can make people feel loved for who they are.

They can also open my heart, refocus me, refocus my heart, and change my thinking. But on the other hand, my words can:

Burst someone's bubble.

Wreck someone's day.

Crush someone's dream.

Hurt or wound someone's heart.

They say it's good to think before you speak. But, maybe even better, ask Holy Spirit before you speak.

As Proverbs 18:21 says: *"Death and life are in the power of the tongue, and those who love it will eat of its fruit."* What are your words doing?

Think about it…are your words giving life, or are they giving death?

JOY PHARO

I was born on the beautiful island of Hawaii, which is one of the most exquisite places to be raised. As a child, I had severe asthma and lived half of my childhood in the hospital. At the age of ten, I went into cardiac arrest, and...

I died.

I was dead for over an hour. I left my body.

As I was ascending along my journey to heaven, an angel stopped me and said, "You need to go back, it's not your time yet. God has more for you to do." At that very moment, the powerful vibrating light of Jesus, His Resurrection Power, shot through my heart! Immediately, I sat straight up on the gurney and I started pulling out all of the wires and tubes that were attached to my arms and chest. I was perfectly fine.

That day, God had rescued me from death.

God has been faithful to me my whole life. Through death, loss, divorce, sickness, and so many other things that life brought, He has been the one constant presence. Always steadfast and true. He rescued me and allowed me to live so that I could proclaim that He is my God, and He is your God.

God redeemed my life out of divorce and gave me an amazing husband. We have six beautiful children between us, along with their spouses and ten beautiful grandchildren, (soon to be eleven!) They are truly our reward from God's hand.

From death to life, from destruction to restoration, from despair to hope; God is a way maker, and God is unconditionally faithful.

My prayer is that as you read the stories from the scroll within my heart, you will know God's love for you. You see, He is writing the scroll of your life, and Jesus is the only one who is worthy to open it. Revelation 5:4.

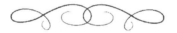

METAMORPHOSIS

Therefore, if anyone is in Christ, he is a new creation; old things have passed away;
behold, all things have become new.
2 Corinthians 5:17 NKJ

The Lord reminded me today of a beautiful memory from my childhood. I was born and raised in Hawaii, so there were a lot of beautiful memories to recall. This memory, though, was profound and literally transforming.

I was around five years old, and I was fascinated with caterpillars, cocoons, and butterflies. It was springtime and caterpillar season in Hawaii. I remember watching the caterpillars for hours crawling on the tree branches. These branches were a display of the different processes of a caterpillar. Some were crawling, some were cocooning.

One day, as I was bounding out the door to play, I spotted a cocoon on the ground attached to a twig. The twig must have broken off from the tree, and the wind plopped it down close to my dad's old Chevy Station Wagon. I thought to myself, *Oh no, it's going to get hurt out here!* Somehow, I instinctively knew not to touch it. So, I shielded it with a makeshift cardboard fence and told my family to be careful around the cocoon.

I kept watch on this cocoon for days. Each day came with many dangers surrounding this helpless cocoon. I remembered it rained one day, my dad almost ran over it with his car another day, and one of my siblings nearly fell on top of it. Each day brought precarious circumstances encircling this cocoon. But I continued to keep watch.

And then, a miracle happened.

I had just come outside to check on my cocoon. At that very moment, it was breaking forth from its cocoon and transformed into a beautiful butterfly! The butterfly flew above my head, rested on my shoulder, and flew away. It was such an unforgettable, profound moment in my life.

God used this experience to show me that we are like these beautiful butterflies. We are born into this world, a world with many perils, tribulations, and precarious circumstances. It is through Him keeping watch over us that we are sustained. God never slumbers or sleeps, but His eyes are continually on us. When we come to the saving knowledge of who Jesus is, God in the flesh, He begins to transform us. We are now a new creation in Him, and He begins to transform us by the renewing of our minds.

We began as little caterpillars, crawling on the Branch, (He is the Branch). He cocooned us in His love, and through His love, He has transformed us into beautiful butterflies. We have gone from crawling on the Branch, to soaring with the wind of His Holy Spirit. The metamorphosis is complete.

"For in Him, we have been made complete, and He is the head over all rule and authority." Colossians 2:10.

Today, as you ponder on the love of God, my prayer is that you may know His joy and that your joy may be complete.

Soar beautiful butterfly, soar!

THE INCORRUPTIBLE SEED

Having been born again, not of corruptible seed but incorruptible, through the Word
of God which lives and abides forever.
1 Peter 1:23 NKJ

Today I want to talk to you about two seeds. The Seed of God vs. the Seed of Satan. God's seed is our great inheritance and an integral part of the Great Commission. (Matthew 28:19-20.)

Ever since the beginning of mankind, Satan has tried to corrupt the seed of man. He has viciously sought to annihilate and corrupt the bloodline of Jesus, through sin.

This has been his main objective.

Before the flood, he almost succeeded in this very endeavor. At this time, almost all mankind was corrupt except for the bloodline of Noah. God had to send a flood because of the enemy's corruptible seed, which had infiltrated mankind. The enemy not only tried to corrupt the bloodline through sin but through fallen angels that had come down. But God preserved His bloodline through Noah, which was bloodline of our Messiah, Jesus. Genesis 6:9 says: "*Noah was a righteous man, blameless in his generation. Noah walked with God.*" Noah was righteous not because he was without sin, but because he walked with God. Noah protected his bloodline because he stayed close to the Father, and kept himself and his family's seed pure.

From the beginning, God's everlasting love for us put hostility between Satan and the woman, and between his seed (Satan's seed) and her seed (Jesus' bloodline.) Genesis 3:15 says *"He (Jesus) would crush the enemy's head and the enemy would bruise His (Jesus) heel."*

The good news is that God has preserved His bloodline throughout the ages, and He is still preserving His bloodline through us. Those who receive Jesus as their Lord and their Savior are a part of the Incorruptible Seed.

"We have been born again, not of corruptible seed, but of incorruptible seed, through the living and abiding Word of God." 1 Peter 1:23. Jesus is the Word that became flesh. This incorruptible seed is our inheritance that will never perish, spoil, or fade. We were bought and paid for by the Blood of Christ. We are no longer like those who have an impure bloodline, but we now belong to a pure bloodline. *We are a chosen people, a royal priesthood, a Holy Nation, God's special possession, that we may declare the praises of Him who called us out of darkness into His marvelous light. 1 Peter 2:9.*

Those who receive the Lord Jesus as their Lord and Savior are part of the Incorruptible Seed.

We are of His Holy bloodline!

We are the Apple of God's eye! In Zechariah 2:8, it says, *"This is what the Lord Almighty says: "After the Glorious One sent me to the nations who have plundered you—for whoever touches you, touches the apple of His eye."* God will not have His seed corrupted, and He is preserving us. We are His Apple seeds.

We are now sowing this incorruptible seed to all those who desperately need a Savior. Every seed that we sow and is harvested will become another believer, and the Apple of God's eye. Alleluia!

Go, go, go, and sow this incorruptible seed! There is a mighty harvest that is ready to be reaped!

A PRAYER FOR YOU

FATHER, MAY YOUR BRIDE AND REMNANT SOW
MUCH SEED AS WE DO THE WORK OF THE KINGDOM.
MAY EACH ONE OF US MOVE IN THE ANOINTING AND
WITH THE SEED THAT YOU PLANTED INTO OUR HEARTS.
MAY WE WALK IN THE LANE THAT
YOU HAVE CALLED US TO WALK IN, AND MAY
WE BRING FORTH MUCH FRUIT FOR YOUR KINGDOM.
WE THANK YOU THAT WE HAVE BEEN BORN AGAIN
OF YOUR INCORRUPTIBLE SEED, THROUGH THE
LIVING AND ABIDING WORD OF GOD.
WE PRAISE YOU, GOD, THAT WE ARE THE APPLE OF YOUR EYE,
A ROYAL PRIESTHOOD, AND A HOLY NATION.
IN JESUS NAME, AMEN!

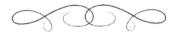

DEFINING LOVE

For God so loved the world that He gave His only begotten Son, that whoever
believes in Him should not perish but have everlasting life.
John 3:16 KJV

L ove.

What is it?

Can love be defined? Can our five senses touch, smell, taste, hear, and see love? Does love have a name?

The answer is yes, and these questions can be answered with scripture.

"For God so loved the world, that He sent His only begotten Son, that whosoever believes in Him, shall not perish, but shall have everlasting life." (John 3:16.)

"For unto us a Child is born, unto us a Son is given; and the government will be upon His shoulder. And His name will be called Wonderful, Counselor, Mighty God, Everlasting Father, and Prince of Peace." (Isaiah 9:6.)

"Behold, a virgin shall be with child and shall bring forth a son, and they shall call His name Emmanuel, which being interpreted is, God with us." (Matthew 1:23.)

"The Word became flesh and made His dwelling among us. We have seen His Glory, the Glory of the One and only Son, who came from the Father, full of grace and truth." (John 1:14.)

God is love, and His definition of love is Jesus.

Therefore, love truly does have a name. The name of love is the name of Jesus! Emanuel, God with us.

God came to live with us one blessed night, so that the world would know how much He loved us. He knew that we needed a Savior. God knew that we needed to touch, smell, taste, hear, and see His love. He stepped out of Glory and came down to earth to redeem us from the curse of sin and death. Jesus took up our pain and bore our sufferings. He made himself nothing, taking the form of a servant, being born in the likeness of men.

Philippians 2:7 says: *"Fully God and Fully Man. For we do not have a High Priest who is unable to sympathize and understand our weaknesses and temptations, but One who has been tempted [knowing exactly how it feels to be human] in every respect as we are, yet without [committing any] sin."* Hebrews 4:15 says*: "Everything that God does is in the name of love."*

Let me describe how God saturates our five senses with His love, through scripture: *"And this will be a sign for you: you will find a baby wrapped in swaddling clothes and lying in a manger."* (Luke 2:12.)

Touch: Matthew 20:24 *"Moved with compassion, Jesus touched their eyes; and immediately, they regained their sight and followed Him."*

Smell: Ephesians 5:2 *"Walk in love, just as Christ also loved you and gave Himself up for us, an offering and a sacrifice to God as a fragrant aroma."*

Taste: Psalm 34:8 *"O taste and see that the LORD is good. How blessed is the man who takes refuge in Him!"*

Sound: John 5:25 *"Truly, truly, I say to you, an hour is coming, and is now here when the dead will hear the voice of the Son of God, and those who hear will live."*

Sight: Matthew 5:8 *"Blessed are the pure in heart, for they shall see God."*

This beautiful baby, sent by God, who *is* God, saturated all of our senses. The preciousness of that one moment, the touch of His hand, the smell of His skin, the taste of His lips, the hearing of His cries, and seeing Emanuel, God with us, a baby in a manger, this *is* love.

God is love.

As we remember the birth of our Lord Jesus Christ, Savior, and King, may we all grasp the magnitude of His love. May we be those who walk in His Love and share His love with those who are perishing, are broken-hearted, and rejected. *"For God so loved the world, that He sent His only begotten Son, that whosoever believes in Him, shall not perish, but shall have everlasting life."* (John 3:16.)

BAPTISM OF FIRE

I (John the Baptist), indeed baptize you with water unto repentance, but He (The Messiah) who is coming after me is mightier than I, whose sandals I am not worthy to carry. He will baptize you with the Holy Spirit and fire.
Matthew 3:11 NKJ

Precious comrades in the Holy Spirit, I want you to know that you are so loved. God loves watching your devotion and your dedication to Him. God loves to see His glory manifested through all of you and He loves watching each one of you use the gifts He has given you through His Holy Spirit. He always wants to expand our capacity and to mature us in Him. With that said, I believe that He is bringing His Bride into deeper waters.

The Lord has been teaching me about the Baptism of the Holy Spirit and the Baptism of Fire. We were all baptized in the Holy Spirit when we were saved, born again. God bestowed His gifts to us and through us. Each one of us is the evidence of that precious miracle and gift. In Him, you move, live, and have your being. He gave us these gifts for our lives to be full of Him and to be a witness of Him to many lives. That is why He baptized us with His Holy Spirit. Alleluia! It is a witness of Him in us.

Now, I believe that the Lord is teaching us to move with His power and authority. God is bringing us into an immersed intimacy and reverent consecration with Him. As we consecrate ourselves to Him through fasting and obedience, not as an act of works, but through an act of faith and love for Him, He is working into our lives, sanctification, purification, and holiness. This process of sanctification can only be done through the Baptism of Fire. It's an ongoing process, and it is a witness of our maturity in Him as a Christian. It's the higher call, the deeper depth. In this process of Baptism of Fire, all the impurities will be flushed away, and what remains will be a pearl of great price, a precious jewel for our King's crown.

He is calling us to an epic love story with Him, a divine love story. He is bringing us to a place that the only one we will see in the room is Him, our Lover, our Best friend, our King, our Savior. Through this Baptism of Fire, we will find real intimacy with the Lover of our souls.

It's a higher place. He will increase and we will decrease. In this process of sanctification comes so much victory and so much supernatural power. We will know the heart of the Father, the mind of the Spirit, and the love of the Son. We will be living testimonies of this great Truth. Jesus is the Truth, the Way, and the Life.

He is calling us to an epic love story with Him, a divine love story.

I am cheering all of you on as we journey together on this road of sanctification. May you be so encouraged, and may you look ahead to the joy that is set before you.

God loves all of you so much! Love and blessings to each one of you!

SOUNDS OF SORROW
(S.O.S.)

Surely He has borne our griefs and carried our sorrows...
Isaiah 53:4a NKJ

As I pen the words to this scroll, my heart is broken. Recently, we lost our one-year-old nephew, Leland, to S.I.D.S. It was unexpected, it was sudden. When I received the news, I heard myself utter, "What?! NO! How?" I could hear the shock in my voice. I heard the guttural sound of anguish breaking the silence. I heard the agony in my niece's voice, as she delivered this heartbreaking, dreadful news over the phone.

Yes, sorrow has a sound.

The sounds of sorrow are likened to the abbreviation S.O.S. An S.O.S. is a flashing distress signal by Morse code for ships in distress. Morse code was used with dots and dashes, and it was repeated at brief intervals to relay that their ship was in jeopardy.

The sound of our sorrow is a distress signal to God. Our ship is sinking; the waves of absolute despair have beaten us down. We cry out to God with overwhelming emotion. We utter words of extreme sadness and the watershed of tears begin to flow. Our tears are the dots and the dashes of our sorrow and despair.

God apprehends our grief; His ears are attentive to our cries. He hears the smallest whimper or our deepest rasping of pain.

Life, at times, can be so hard. There are different circumstances like death—especially the death of a child—divorce, financial loss, loss of friendship, the list is endless, and they all bring despair. Each one of these sorrows has a sound.

Amid so much sorrow, I am comforted that my cries and pain have a place of refuge, a place to navigate into a safe harbor, and that safe harbor is in the arms of my Savior, Jesus Christ. He is my comfort and my hope. I have a hope that cannot be extinguished or diminished by the sounds of sorrow.

I want to throw a life preserver out to you, and this life preserver has a name; His name is Jesus. If you are experiencing hopelessness and desperation, have solace in this: Jesus is guarding our hearts and our minds in this place of anguish and despair. He is holding us above the water and has promised to wipe away every tear from our eyes. There will be no more death, mourning, crying, or pain in heaven, when He will make all things new again. We have a living hope, an inheritance of hope that will never perish, spoil, or fade.

Have solace in this; Jesus is guarding your heart and your mind in this place of anguish and despair.

He is our hope.

Psalm 46:1 says: *"God is our refuge and strength, an ever-present help in trouble."* He is there to comfort us and bring us through our grief. He is the Captain of our sinking ship, and He hears the sounds of our sorrow. He will always respond to our S.O.S. He is our comfort in our suffering. He is our Lifeguard. His promises preserve us. He is sovereign and in control. We will never drown in our tears of sorrow, for He is with us always. Nothing; life or death, good or bad, gain or loss, happiness or pain, will ever separate us from His love.

My comfort is that I know Jesus heard the sound of sorrow on the cross. He took up our pain and bore our suffering by His wounds, and we are healed. He heard my sounds of sorrow; he hears your sounds of sorrow. He has heard the S.O.S. of our hearts, and He will always comfort us. Selah.

In loving memory of

Leland Perci McCreadie

April 1ˢᵗ, 2018 – May 16ᵗʰ, 2019

You impacted all of our lives, in so many beautiful ways!

Remembering you and your laughter,

ALWAYS and FOREVER!

THE THRESHOLD COVENANT

Jesus said, "I am the door. If anyone enters by Me, he will be saved, and he will go in and out and find pasture.
John 10:9 NKJ

In an article written by Messianic Jewish Rabbi, Zev Porat, he spoke about the Threshold Covenant and it catapulted me back to an experience I had with my Aunty Pat as she was transitioning from life to death, to eternal life.

He wrote that in times of Israel's antiquity, houses were built with a threshold under the doorframe of the house. It had a special sanctity. The threshold was made of stone and was cut slightly higher than the floor, so water and dirt could be kept out. There was a bowl carved into the threshold for blood to spill into. In ancient times, when Israelites would enter into a covenant of trust and honor with someone, the host of the house would invite them to their house and sacrifice a kosher animal on the threshold of their home. They would let the blood spill into the bowl that was carved into the threshold. The person who they were making a covenant with, would take a step over the threshold, and they were careful to not touch the blood. It was an act of accepting a covenant with you.

This is what Jesus did for us.

Exodus 12:22 says: *"And you will take a hyssop branch, and dip it in the blood that is in the threshold and strike the lintel and the two side posts with the blood that is in the threshold, and none of you will go out at the door until the morning."*

Jesus is our Savior, by His shed blood on the cross (the doorway), we are saved. Jesus is the Door. *"I am the Door: by Me, if any man enters in, he shall be saved, and shall go in and out and find pasture."* (John 10:9.)

I recently had the honor of being with my Aunty Pat and taking care of her in her last week of life on Earth. What a sad, but amazingly beautiful week I had with her!

As she was transitioning between here and heaven, she would slip into periods of sleep and wake up to tell me and my Aunty Joanne, her sister, glorious things! In one of those moments when she came back from one of her journeys with Jesus, she told us that everything was fixed. They say when people are in the dying process that they are journeying and working things out. She also said that there's a door and it's rising up, (she was in the "Jesus elevator!") On the other side of the door, there was so much food! She was allowed to taste some and she said it was the best food she had ever tasted in her life. She also told us that this food had not been eaten by people yet, but it was waiting to be distributed.

> **Jesus is our Savior, by His shed blood on the cross, we are saved.**

The door was rising up! My Aunty loved Jesus, and He said to her, *"Here I am! I stand at the door and knock, Pat. You have heard My voice, and you have opened the door. I will come in and eat with you, and you with Me!"* My Aunty stepped over the threshold into Glory. The sacrificial blood of Jesus covered the threshold. She was covenanted to Jesus, and like a groom with His bride, He carried her over the threshold! Alleluia!

As the Bride of Christ, we are covenanted to our Groom Jesus. It gives me such peace to know that as we pass from this life to be forever with our Savior, He is waiting to carry us over the threshold.

MEGAN STOCKWELL

I was raised in a Christian home, and at the age of twelve, my parents divorced. There was so much going on internally and externally, that it fueled thoughts of rejection and that I had to "earn" attention—especially from male figures—to feel accepted.

As I grew up, I chased romantic relationships to feel complete. I was pregnant at eighteen, then married, and went through a terrible divorce by the age of twenty-two. I found myself at the lowest of lows. Guys, alcohol, bars, friends, work, being a single mom; nothing was fulfilling that deep ache in my heart from the rejection, shame, and loneliness that my own choices had brought.

I attended a women's conference where, for the first time in a long time, I felt the love of Jesus wash over me. Then, a song was sung over me: "You are so beautiful...to me...can't you see! You're everything

I've hoped for, you're everything I need...You are so beautiful....to me!" I cried and cried and cried. The wounds that were open and exposed started to heal. I realized that the external affection from a man or anyone else would never feel the same as the internal love of Jesus that covers all pain and heartache.

A few years later, I was going to church, serving on the worship team and I started dating the "perfect" guy. A short while later, an exposed wound was re-opened and I found myself going down the dangerous "what-if" road.

One day, while on stage during worship, I prayed, "God, tell me what to do! I will do anything!" Just then, a stranger approached me—on stage—and told me she had a word for me. I thought to myself, *Ok? Just get on with it.*

The woman said to me, "I don't know what this means, but I just keep hearing *'he's the one!'"*

It was the answer that I had been praying for.

At that very moment, I felt God's tangible love and I knew God had heard my prayers. To know that God saw me was a life-changing, literally a light switch moment for me.

I'm now married to that "perfect" guy, with two beautiful boys. I'm a huge advocate for sharing God's love and helping others see how He loves them, and knows them!

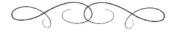

INTIMACY WITH JESUS

God is love.
1 John 4:16b NKJ

Intimacy: *a close familiarity or friendship; Closeness.*
Love: *an intense feeling or affection.*

God is the very essence of love. We desire to know Him, and we crave the intimacy of His closeness, familiarity and friendship. It is through His unconditional love that we find ourselves and our hearts become whole. He is the truest, purest form of a Father.

It is interesting how one experience can change how we set our expectations for future experiences. For example, if you try a new restaurant and the food and experience is amazing, you will surely want to return, but if you go to a new restaurant and the food or service is terrible, you will probably never go back.

Positive and negative experiences can shape our perception and either push us to try new things, or keep us more reserved and not branch out the next time in decision making. A lot of times, when we experience the same good or bad experience over and over again, we begin to see the fruit of how it can shape our decisions, whether it be consciously or subconsciously.

This can be applied to how we view God as a Father. The definition of a father is a male parent or a man who has a child. We experience many different versions of fathers or father figures in our lifetimes.

Some of these experiences could be good and others, unfortunately, are not so good. Sometimes how we view our father, or other father figures on Earth, can make it difficult to understand how God could be a Father to us, with no physical person to touch or see. When your heart desires something, you want to be able to see it, touch it, and feel it.

When it came to my personal relationship with God and accepting Him, the Father that He says He is, it was really difficult for me. Growing up, I experienced rejection on many occasions and on many levels. Distrust and disbelief were always in the forefront of my mind, and I held myself back from Him because of the fear that I would be rejected or worse, unloved.

Some of us grow up thinking of God as only a Heavenly Father who's just a distant figure that we worship and praise. We see Him as a God, a King, and High above all. Most of the time, we do not see Him as a loving, caring, compassionate, sincere daddy who loves you, and cries when you cry, and smiles when you smile, and laughs when you laugh. He wants to be close to you!

Jeremiah 1:5a says: *"He knew us before we were born."* When you know something like that, you want to see it come to fruition. You want to see the end result. Even though God is all-knowing, He desires for us to *choose* Him and to walk with Him.

Intimacy is not *spatial*; it is relational. Meaning that you can have intimacy with someone halfway across the world more so than the person standing next to you. People assume that intimacy means physical closeness. That is just not true. The definition of intimacy is: close familiarity or friendship; closeness.

We must learn to grow our relational intimacy with Jesus; daily, consistently, and unwaveringly.

God thought of us before anyone else did; He knew what we would look like, sound like, be like, and yet sometimes, we don't feel like we know Him at all. Because of our doubts and misconceptions, we do not feel close to Him. He wants for us to know Him as much as He knows us. This doesn't mean to know Him through recognition, but to know Him within your heart.

Sometimes people expect relational intimacy to happen in a metaphoric "relationship microwave." It's hastily placed within; the door is closed and, *Ding!* It's done! This is a misconception. Intimacy and closeness are sown and grown, not pulled out of a container, premade and ready for instant gratification. You must reserve time and spend it with that special person, getting to know them and what speaks to their heart. Gradually, you will learn their character. You will begin to understand why they make the choices they do. Eventually, you can read them like the back of your hand. It is in this way that we must learn to grow our relational intimacy with Jesus; daily, consistently, and unwaveringly.

So, how do we become comfortable having intimacy and closeness with Jesus? Before we start just choosing and doing, we need to have a revelation. A revelation will make it a realization of how this applies to you. Our heart needs to believe it and know it just as much as our head and ears understand it. Once our heart understands this, it will draw you in and you'll desire to learn more about Him. This will lead you to desire to talk with Him. Taking time out of your day, choosing to set aside time for Him, for prayer, worship, and reading His Word, His love will become more real to you. It will not just be a thought in passing, but it will become a truth in your life.

Then, when you hear God speak to you for the first time, and it is confirmed that you really did hear from God, it will leave you wanting to hear Him more. You won't doubt when you hear Him, because you'll just *know* that your Father has spoken to you.

He loves you! He wants to spend time with you, but He wants you to choose Him. Don't we, ourselves, want to feel chosen?

Jeremiah 29:11-13 says: *"For I know the thoughts that I think toward you, says the Lord, thoughts of peace and not evil, to give you a future and a hope. Then you will call upon Me and go and pray to Me, and I will listen. And you will seek Me and find Me, when you search for Me with all your heart."*

1 John 4:18-19 says: *"There is no fear in love; but perfect love casts out fear, because fear involves torment. But he who fears has not been made perfect in love. We love Him because He first loved us."*

NO WORRIES

Jesus said, "Therefore I say to you, do not worry about your life, what you will eat or what you will drink; nor about your body, what you will put on. Is not life more than food and the body more than clothing?"
Matthew 6:25 NKJ

Life is always…going.

The baby needs changing. The kids need to get to school on time with lunches in hand. Rent needs to be paid. The boss wants you to come in early. You are deciding whether or not it's time to move. The Pastor is asking you to serve in a ministry that you don't really want to serve in, but you see the need and know that you could be a huge help…

There is always something to do, and there is always something that comes along with the decision to act, be it positive or negative. In life, we can always find things to decide on, but, do we decide in peace or in worry? Some decisions, like changing the baby, taking the kids to school, and paying rent, must be done and don't require contemplation. Other decisions present you with a choice to make. Sometimes, there isn't a wrong choice, but if you make that choice out of worry instead of peace, there can be adverse side effects.

God does not function in chaos. He does not want you to worry or stress or fear. We know that He is always with us, but sometimes in the mid-day choices, we don't feel like we should approach God with the minor things. Yet, these minor things are creating so much worry in our hearts and soul that it starts to overwhelm us. The word 'worry' means to give way to anxiety and unease. That is not at all the character of our Father God. In Matthew 6, it says, *"Do not worry."*

It doesn't say you *might* not want to worry.

It's telling you *not* to worry. Why?

Because if you trust in God and you know that He wants the best for you, then why should we worry? Easier said than done, right?

> **God does not function in chaos.**

With the help of the Holy Spirit and continual time with Jesus during your day, it will help keep you on the peaceful path. Our emotions are not bad. Our random thoughts are not bad. We need to get to a place where we recognize if that emotion or thought is from God, and if we should continue to let it replay itself in our minds. If not, then it's time to lay it down at Jesus' feet.

Take a moment and ponder the powerful message behind Matthew 10:31: *"So don't be afraid; you are worth more than many sparrows."* And, Psalm 62:1-2: *"Truly my soul finds rest in God; my salvation comes from Him. Truly He is my rock and my salvation; He is my fortress; I will never be shaken."*

Don't ever feel bad when you let yourself worry. We are human. Take a moment for repentance and recognize in your heart that God is good and for you. We need to come to a place where Jesus is the center of our lives. Everything around us can spin out of control, but we choose to not let it consume us.

We choose peace.

We choose Jesus.

SALVATION PRAYER

We cannot earn our salvation; we are saved by God's grace when we have faith in His Son, Jesus Christ. All you need to do is believe you are a sinner and that Christ died for your sins, and ask His forgiveness. Then, turn away from your sins; that's called repentance. Jesus Christ knows you and loves you. What matters to Him is the attitude of your heart and your honesty. We suggest praying the following prayer to accept Christ as your Savior:

DEAR FATHER GOD,
I KNOW I'M A SINNER,
AND I ASK FOR YOUR FORGIVENESS.
I BELIEVE JESUS CHRIST IS YOUR SON.
I BELIEVE THAT YOU, JESUS DIED FOR MY SINS,
AND THAT THREE DAYS LATER YOU WERE RAISED
TO LIFE. I WANT TO TRUST YOU, JESUS, AS MY
SAVIOR AND FOLLOW YOU AS MY LORD, FROM THIS
DAY FORWARD. I INVITE YOU IN AND SURRENDER
MY LIFE COMPLETELY TO YOU.
I PRAY THIS IN THE NAME OF JESUS.
AMEN.

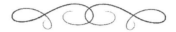

If you would like to know more about a relationship with Jesus, the team from Sanctioned Love would love to talk with you!

www.SanctionedLove.com
P.O. Box 7478, Klamath Falls, OR 97602
Phone: 541-591-1558

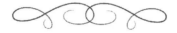

TO OUR READERS

Sanctioned Love would like to thank you for reading the scrolls of our hearts. Now you, the reader, are forever a part of our testimonies. To God be all the glory and honor! *"Rejoice with those who rejoice, weep with those who weep."* (Romans 12:15.)

Sanctioned Love's prayer is that our testimonies brought you laughter, made you smile, and brought you comfort. Our desire for you is that our scrolls from heaven transfigured a moment in your story, and in your scroll. Most of all, we hope that you felt the love that God has for you.

We are forever grateful and humbled. *"I have not stopped giving thanks for you, remembering you in my prayers."* (Ephesians 1:16.)

Love always,

Sanctioned Love

We'd love to hear from you!

Please leave us a review at: **www.Amazon.com**

Check out our Facebook page: **www.FB.com/SanctionedLove**

View our Website: **www.SanctionedLove.com**

A SPECIAL THANKS

With a humble heart, we want to thank Rheyma Oosterman. What started out as a simple book project turned into countless hours and months of coordination, research, cases of Coca-Cola, "computering," and line-editing; you handled everything like a seasoned professional.

Thank you!

There are no words to describe the amount of appreciation and love that these two words contain, but we hope you can see our gratitude shining like a beacon. Without your help, this book wouldn't be what it is today. "*We always thank God, the Father of our Lord Jesus Christ, when we pray for you.*" (Colossians 1:3.) From the bottom of our hearts to the tips of our toes: thank you, thank you, thank you.

Not only have you been a blessing through your help with the book, but God has sent you to us to be an instrument of His Love, and through the Holy Spirit, you've filled our hearts with love. We're so grateful for your presence in our lives.

PMLYTTMAB!

("Pretty much love you to the moon and back!")

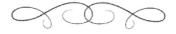

…and a very special thank-you to Kristi Stalder, our editor and our publisher. God specifically chose her and trusted her with this assignment. She heard each one of our hearts and helped us to present our scrolls, as a beautiful masterpiece. God used her as an experienced gardener. She picked the flowers from each of our gardens and made a beautiful bouquet. This book, is that bouquet.

Thank you, Kristi, for your excellence, your expertise, your dedication, and the countless hours you gave so unselfishly. You are the exquisite ribbon on our bouquet. You, "piloted this plane well, as you/we were building it." We are eternally thankful for YOU!

To contact Kristi at Stalder Books & Publishing,
you can connect with her at:

www.KristiStalder.com

Email: **KristiStalder@yahoo.com**

Facebook, Twitter and Instagram: @**AuthorKristiStalder**

Made in the USA
San Bernardino, CA
07 July 2020